THE THEATRE AND ITS DOUBLE

The Theatre and its Double is a collection of essays written by the French poet and playwright, Antonin Artaud. It remains the most radical text on performance in print today. This volume contains both famous Manifestos of the Theatre of Cruelty in which the author sets out the practical applications of his theatre; the definitions of this theatre; the underlying impulses of performance (what Artaud called its metaphysics); some suggestions on a physical training method for actors and actresses; a long appreciation of the expressive values of Eastern dance drama, and much more. Also included for the first time is *Seraphim's Theatre*, where Artaud attempts an actor's application of the Taoist principles of fullness and emptyness. That this text has been used as basic working material by Peter Brook and the Royal Shakespeare Company, by Grotowski's company in Poland and by the Living Theatre, gives some idea of its past influence. It is widely read throughout the world as a source of inspiration for the new drama, for those in search of the meaning of theatre, as well as for the beauty of its lines.

D0582725

NEW PARIS EDITIONS: 1

THE THEATRE AND ITS DOUBLE

essays by

Antonin Artaud

Translated by Victor Corti

CALDER PUBLICATIONS
LONDON

First published in Great Britain in 1970 by
Calder & Boyars Limited
Reprinted 1974

Reprinted in 1977, 1981, 1985 and 1989
John Calder (Publishers) Limited

This edition first published in France in 1993 by
Association Calder

and in Great Britain in 1993 by
Calder Publications Limited
126 Cornwall Road, London SE1 8TQ

Reprinted 1995, 1999

Reprinted by Calder Publications 2001, 2005
Originally published in *Antonin Artaud: Oeuvres Completes Tome IV*
by Editions Gallimard, Paris 1964

© Editions Gallimard 1964
© This translation John Calder (Publishers) Ltd 1970, 1974, 1977, 1981, 1985, 1989
© This translation by Calder Publications Ltd 1993
© Postface by Calder Publications Ltd 1993

ISBN 0 7145 4234 2

British Library Cataloguing-in-Publication Data
A catalogue record of this book is available from the British Library.

Printed and bound in Great Britain by CPI Bath Press, Bath

CONTENTS

THEATRE AND THE PLAGUE

In the archives of the small town of Caligari, Sardinia, lies an account of an astonishing historic occurrence.

One night about the end of April or the beginning of May, 1720, some twenty days before the ship *Grand-Saint-Antoine* reached Marseilles, where its landing coincided with the most wondrous outbreak of plague that erupted throughout the city's archives, Saint-Rémys, the Sardinian Viceroy, perhaps rendered more sensitive to that most baleful virus by his restricted monarchical duties, had a particularly agonising dream. He saw himself plague-ridden and saw the disease ravage his tiny state.

Society's barriers became fluid with the effects of the scourge. Order disappeared. He witnessed the subversion of all morality, the breakdown of all psychology, heard his lacerated, utterly routed bodily fluids murmur within him in a giddy wasting away of matter, they grew heavy and were then gradually transformed into carbon. Was it too late to ward off the scourge? Although organically destroyed, crushed, extirpated, his very bones consumed, he knew one does not die in dreams, that our will-power even operates *ad absurdum,* even denying what is possible, in a kind of metamorphosis of lies reborn as truth.

He awoke. He would show himself able to drive away these plague rumours and the miasmas of the Oriental virus.

The *Grand-Saint-Antoine,* a month out of Beyreut, requested permission to enter the harbour and dock there. At this point the Viceroy gave an insane order, an order thought raving mad, absurd, stupid and despotic both by his subjects and his suite. He hastily dispatched a pilot's boat and men to the supposedly infected vessel with orders for the *Grand-Saint-Antoine* to tack about that instant and make full sail away from the town or be sunk by cannon shot. War on the plague. The autocrat did not do things by halves.

In passing, we ought to note the unusually influential power the dream exerted on him, since it allowed him to insist on the savage fierceness of his orders despite the gibes of the populace and the scepticism of his suite, when to do so meant riding roughshod not only over human rights, but even over the most ordinary respect for life, over all kinds of national and international conventions, which in the face of death, no longer apply.

Be that as it may, the ship held her course, made land at Leghorn and sailed into Marseilles roads where she was allowed to dock.

The Marseilles authorities have kept no record of what happened to her plague-infected cargo. We roughly know what happened to the members of her crew; they did not all die of the plague but were scattered over various countries.

The *Grand-Saint-Antoine* did not bring the plague to Marseilles, it was already there, at a particular stage of renewed activity, but its centres had been successfully localised.

The plague brought by the *Grand-Saint-Antoine* was the original, Oriental virus, hence the unusually horrible aspect, the widespread flaring up of the epidemic, and dates from its arrival and dispersion throughout the town.

This prompts a few thoughts.

This plague, which apparently revived a virus, was able to wreak as great havoc on its own, since the Captain was the only member of the ship's crew who did not catch the plague. Then again it did not seem that the newly arrived infected men had ever

8

been in direct contact with those others confined to their quarantine districts. The *Grand-Saint-Antoine* passed within hailing distance of Caligari, Sardinia, but did not leave the plague there, yet the Viceroy picked up certain of its emanations in his dreams. For one cannot deny that a substantial though subtle communication was established between the plague and himself. It is too easy to lay the blame for communication of such a disease on infection by contact alone.

But this communication between Saint-Rémys and the plague, though of sufficient intensity to release imagery in his dreams, was after all not powerful enough to infect him with the disease.

Nevertheless, the town of Caligari, learning some time later that the ship driven from its shores by the miraculously enlightened though despotic Prince's will was the cause of the great Marseilles epidemic, recorded the fact in its archives where anyone may find it.

The 1720 Marseilles plague has given us what may pass as the only clinical description we have of the scourge.

But one wonders whether the plague described by Marseilles doctors was exactly the same as the 1347 Florence epidemic which produced the *Decameron*. Histories and holy books, the Bible among them, certain old medical treatises, describe the outward symptoms of all kinds of plagues whose malignant features seem to have impressed them far less than the demoralising and prodigious effect they produced in their minds. No doubt they were right, for medicine would be hard put to establish any basic difference between the virus Pericles died of before Syracuse (if the word virus is anything more than a verbal convenience) and that appearing in the plague described by Hippocrates, which, as recent medical treatises inform us, are a kind of fictitious plague. These same treatises hold the only genuine plague comes from Egypt, arising from the cemeteries uncovered by the subsiding Nile. The Bible and Herodotus both call attention to the lightning appearance

9

of a plague that decimated 180,000 men of the Assyrian army in one night, thereby saving the Egyptian Empire. If this fact is true, we ought to consider the scourge as the immediate medium or materialisation of a thinking power in close contact with what we call fate.

This, with or without the army of rats that hurled itself on the Assyrian troops that night, and gnawed away their accoutrements in a few hours. The above event ought to be compared with the epidemic that broke out in 660 B.C. in the Holy City of Mekao, Japan, on the occasion of a mere change of government.

The 1502 Provence plague, which gave Nostradamus his first opportunity to practise his powers of healing, also coincided with the most profound political upheavals, the downfall or death of kings, the disappearance and destruction of whole provinces, earthquakes, all kinds of magnetic phenomena, exodus of the Jews, proceeding or following on disasters or havoc of a political or cosmic order, those causing them being too idiotic to foresee them, or not really depraved enough to desire their after effects.

However mistaken historians or doctors may have been about the plague I think one might agree on the idea of the disease as a kind of psychic entity, not carried by a virus. If we were to analyse closely all the facts on contagious plagues given in history or con- tained in archives, we would have difficulty in singling out one properly established occurrence of contagious contact, and the example Boccaccio cites of swine that died because they sniffed at sheets in which the plague-ridden had been wrapped scarcely suggests more than a kind of strange affinity between swine-flesh and the nature of the plague, something which would have to be gone into very thoroughly.

Since the concept of a truly morbid entity does not exist, there are forms the mind can provisionally agree on to designate certain phenomena, and it seems our minds might agree on a plague described in the following manner.

Before any pronounced physical or psychological sickness

appears, red spots appear all over the body, the sick person only suddenly noticing them when they turn black. He has no time to be alarmed by them before his head feels on fire, grows overwhelmingly heavy and he collapses. Then he is seized with terrible fatigue, a focal, magnetic, exhausting tiredness, his molecules are split in two and drawn towards their annihilation. His fluids wildly jumbled in disorder, seem to race though his body. His stomach heaves, his insides seem to want to burst out between his teeth. His pulse sometimes slows down until it becomes a shadow, a latent pulse, at other times it races in accordance with his seething inner fever, the streaming wanderings of his mind. His pulse beating as fast as his heart, growing intense, heavy, deafening; those eyes, first inflamed, then glazed. That hugely swollen panting tongue, first white, then red, then black, as if charred and cracked, all heralding unprecedented organic disturbances. Soon the fluids, furrowed like the earth by lightning, like a volcano tormented by subterranean upheavals, seek an outlet. Fiery cones are formed at the centre of each spot and around them the skin rises up in blisters like air bubbles under a skin of lava. These blisters are surrounded by rings, the outer one, just like Saturn's ring at maximum radiance, indicating the outer edge of the bubo.

The body is streaked with them. Just as volcanoes have their own chosen locations on earth, the bubos have their own chosen spots over the expanse of the human body. Bubos appear around the anus, under the armpits, at those precious places where the active glands steadily carry out their functions, and through these bubos the anatomy discharges either its inner putrefaction, or in other cases, life itself. A violent burning sensation localised in one spot, more often than not indicates that the life force has lost none of its strengh and that abatement of the sickness or even a cure may be possible. Like silent rage, the most terrible plague is one that does not disclose its symptoms.

Once open, a plague victim's body exhibits no lesions. The gall bladder, which filters heavier, solid organic waste, is full, swollen

11

to bursting point with a sticky black liquid, so dense it suggests new matter. Arterial and veinal blood is also black and sticky. The body is as hard as stone. On the walls of the stomach membrane countless blood sources have arisen and everything points to a basic disorder in secretion. But there is neither loss nor destruction as in leprosy or syphilis. The intestines themselves, the site of the bloodiest disorders, where matter reaches an unbelievable degree of decomposition and calcification, are not organically affected. The gall bladder, from which the hardest matter must be virtually torn as in some human sacrifices, with a sharp knife, an obsidian instrument, hard and glazed – the gall bladder is hypertrophied and fragile in places, yet intact, without an iota missing, any visible lesions or loss of matter.

However, in some cases, the lesioned brain and lungs blacken and become gangrenous. The softened, chopped up lungs fall in chips of an unknown black substance, the brain fissured, crushed and disintegrated, is reduced to powder, to a kind of coal black dust.

Two notable observations can be made about the above facts. The first is that the plague syndrome is complete without any gangrene in the lungs or brain and the plague victim dies without any putrefaction in his limbs. Without underestimating the disease, the anatomy does not need localised physical gangrene to make up its mind to die.

The second remark is that the only two organs really affected and injured by the plague, the brain and lungs, are both dependant on consciousness or the will. We can stop breathing or thinking, speed up our breath, induce any rhythm we choose, make it conscious or unconscious at will, bring about a balance between both kinds of breathing; automatic, under direct control of the sympathetic nerve, and the other, which obeys each new conscious mental reflex.

We can also speed up, slow down or accent our thoughts. We can regulate the subconscious interplay of the mind. We cannot control the filtering of the fluids by the liver, the redistribution of the blood within the anatomy, by the heart and arteries, control digestion, stop or speed up the elimination of substances in the intestines. Hence the plague seems to make its presence known in those places, to have a liking for all those physical localities where human will-power, consciousness and thought are at hand or in a position to occur.

During the 1880's, a French doctor called Yersin, working on the corpses of Indo-Chinese who had died of the plague, isolated one of these round-headed, short-tailed bacilli only visible under a microscope, and called it the plague microbe. In my eyes, this is only a much smaller, infinitely smaller material factor, which appears at any moment during the development of the virus, but does not help to explain the plague at all. And I would rather this doctor had told me why all great plagues last five months, with or without a virus, after which the virulence dies down, and how the Turkish Ambassador passing through Languedoc towards the end of 1720 could draw an imaginary line from Nice to Bordeaux passing through Avignon and Toulouse, as the outer geographic limit of the scourge's spread, events having proved him correct.

From the above it is apparent that the disease has a mental physiognomy whose laws cannot be scientifically specified and it would be useless to try and fix its geographic source, since Egyptian plague is not Oriental plague, nor is it Hippocrates', nor that of Syracuse, nor that in Florence, nor the Black Death which accounted for fifty million lives in medieval Europe. No one can say why the plague strikes a fleeing coward and spares a rake satisfying himself on the corpses of the dead. Why isolation, chastity or solitude are ineffectual against the scourge's attacks or why a group of debauchees who have retired to the countryside, such as Boccaccio, his two well-equipped companions and their seven lustful devotees, could calmly await the hot weather when the plague subsides. Or why in a nearby castle, turned into a warlike fortress ringed with troops barring anyone from entering, the plague turned the garrison and all the occupants into corpses yet spared the guards, alone exposed to infection. Equally, who could explain why the sanitary cordons set up with great numbers of troops by Mahmet Ali about the end of the last century at the time of a fresh outbreak of Egyptian plague, effectively protected convents, schools, prisons and palaces. And that many plague epidemics with all the characteristics of Oriental plague, could suddenly have broken out in medieval Europe in those parts without any contact with the East.

Out of these peculiarities, mysteries, contradictions and traits, we ought to be able to construct the mental features of a disease which saps the anatomy and life, until it is torn apart and causes spasms, like pain which, as it intensifies, strikes deeper, increases its resources and means of access in every ramification of our sensibility.

But out of the mental freedom with which the plague evolves, without any rats, germs or contact, we can deduce the dark, ultimate action of a spectacle I am going to try and analyse.

Once the plague is established in a city, normal social order collapses. There is no more refuse collection, no more army, police or municipality. Pyres are lit to burn the dead whenever men are available. Each family wants its own. Then wood, space and fire grow scarce, families fight around the pyres, soon to be followed by general flight since there are too many corpses. The streets are already choked with crumbling pyramids of the dead, the vermin gnawing at the edges. The stench rises in the air like tongues of flame. Whole streets are blocked by mounds of dead. Then the houses are thrown open and raving plague victims disperse through the streets howling, their minds full of horrible visions. The disease gnawing at their vitals, running through their whole anatomy, is discharged in mental outbursts. Other plague victims who, without bubos or delirium, pain or rashes, examine themselves proudly in

14

the mirror, feeling in splendid health, only to fall dead with their shaving dishes in their hands, full of scorn for other victims.

Over the thick, bloody, noxious streaming gutters, the colour of anguish and opium, spirting from the corpses, strange men clothed in wax, with noses a mile long and glass eyes, mounted on kinds of Japanese sandals made up of a double arrangement of wooden slabs, a horizontal one in the form of a sole, with the uprights isolating them from the infected liquids, pass by chanting absurd litanies, though their sanctity does not prevent them falling into the holocaust in turn. These ignorant doctors only show their fear and childishness.

The scum of the populace, immunised so it seems by their frantic greed, enter the open houses and help themselves to riches they know will serve no purpose or profit. At this point, theatre establishes itself. Theatre, that is to say that momentary pointlessness which drives them to useless acts without immediate profit.

The remaining survivors go berserk; the virtuous and obedient son kills his father, the continent sodomise their kin. The lewd become chaste. The miser chucks handfuls of his gold out of the windows, the Soldier Hero sets fire to the town he had formerly risked his life to save. Dandies deck themselves out and stroll among the charnel-houses. Neither a concept of lack of sanctions nor one of imminent death are enough to motivate such pointlessly absurd acts among people who did not believe death could end anything. How else can we explain that upsurge of erotic fever among the recovered victims who, instead of escaping, stay behind, seeking out and snatching sinful pleasure from the dying or even the dead, half crushed under the pile of corpses where chance had lodged them.

But if a major scourge is needed to make this frenzied pointlessness appear and if that scourge is called the plague, we might perhaps attempt to determine the value of this pointlessness in relation to our whole personality. The condition of a plague victim who dies without any material destruction, yet with all the stigmata

15

of an absolute, almost abstract disease upon him, is in the same condition as an actor totally penetrated by feelings without any benefit or relation to reality. Everything in the actor's physical aspect, just as in the plague victim, shows life has reacted to a paroxysm, yet nothing has happened.

Between the shrieking plague-ridden who run in pursuit of their imaginings, and actors in pursuit of their sensibility, between a living man who invents characters he would never have thought of dreaming up without the plague, bringing them to life amidst an audience of corpses and raving lunatics, and the poet who inopportunely invents characters entrusting them to an equally inert or delirious audience, there are other analogies which account for the only important truths, placing theatre action like that of the plague, on a par with a true epidemic.

Whereas plague imagery related to an advanced state of physical disorganisation is like the last outbursts of waning mental strength, the imagery of poetry in the theatre is a mental power which begins its trajectory in the tangible and gets along without reality. Once launched in fury, an actor needs infinitely more virtue to stop himself committing a crime, than a murderer needs to perpetrate his crime, and this is where, in their pointlessness, these acts of stage feeling appear as something infinitely more valid than those feelings worked out in life.

Compared with a murderer's fury that exhausts itself, a tragic actor's remains enclosed with a circle. The murderer's anger has accomplished an act, and is released, losing contact with the power that inspired, but will no longer sustain it. The actor's has assumed a form that denies itself progressively as it is released, merging with universality.

If we are now prepared to accept this mental picture of the plague, we can consider the plague victim's disturbed fluids as a solidified, substantial aspect of a disorder which on other levels is equivalent to the clashes, struggles, disasters and devastation brought about by events. Just as it is not impossible that the un-

16

consumed despair of a lunatic screaming in an asylum can cause the plague, so by a kind of reversibility of feelings and imagery, in the same way we can admit that outward events, political conflicts, natural disasters, revolutionary order and wartime chaos, when they occur on a theatre level are released into the audience's sensitivity with the strength of an epidemic.

In *The City of God*, St. Augustine points to the similarity of the plague which kills without destroying any organs and theatre which without killing, induces the most mysterious changes not only in the minds of individuals but in a whole nation.

"Know then," he writes, "you who are ignorant of this, that these plays, exhibitions of shameless folly and licence, were established at Rome not by the vicious craving of men but by the appointment of your gods. Much more pardonably might you have rendered divine honours to Scipio* than to gods such as these; indeed, the gods were not so moral as their pontiff! . . .

"They enjoined that plays be exhibited in their honour to stay a physical pestilence, while their pontiff prohibited the theatre to prevent a moral pestilence. If then there remains in you sufficient mental enlightenment to prefer the soul to the body, choose whom you will worship. But these astute and wicked spirits, foreseeing that in due course the pestilence would shortly cease, took occasion to infect not the bodies, but the morals of their worshippers, with a far more serious disease. And in this plague these gods found great enjoyment because it benighted the minds of men with so gross a darkness and dishonoured them with so foul a deformity, that even quite recently some of those who fled from the sack of Rome and found refuge in Carthage were so infected with the disease that day after day they seemed to contend with one another who should most madly run after the actors in the theatre."

There is no point in trying to give exact reasons for this infectious madness. It would be as much use trying to find reasons

* Scipio Nasica, High Pontiff, who ordered that the theatres in Rome be razed to the ground and their cellars filled.

why the nervous system after a certain time is in tune with the vibrations of the subtlest music and is eventually somehow lastingly modified by it. Above all we must agree stage acting is a delirium like the plague, and is communicable.

The mind believes what it sees and does what it believes; that is the secret of fascination. And in his book, St. Augustine does not doubt the reality of this fascination for one moment.

Yet conditions must be found to give birth to a spectacle that can fascinate the mind. It is not just a matter of art.

For if theatre is like the plague, this is not just because it acts on large groups and disturbs them in one and the same way. There is both something victorious and vengeful in theatre just as in the plague, for we clearly feel that spontaneous fire the plague lights as it passes by is nothing but a gigantic liquidation.

Such a complete social disaster, such organic disorder overflowing with vice, this kind of wholesale exorcism constricting the soul, driving it to the limit, indicates the presence of a condition which is an extreme force and where all the powers of nature are newly rediscovered the instant something fundamental is about to be accomplished.

The plague takes dormant images, latent disorder and suddenly carries them to the point of the most extreme gestures. Theatre also takes gestures and develops them to the limit. Just like the plague, it reforges the links between what does and does not exist in material nature. It rediscovers the idea of figures and archetypal symbols which act like sudden silences, fermata, heart stops, adrenalin calls, incendiary images surging into our abruptly woken minds. It restores all our dormant conflicts and their powers, giving these powers names we acknowledge as signs. Here a bitter clash of symbols takes place before us, hurled one against the other in an inconceivable riot. For theatre can only happen the moment the inconceivable really begins, where poetry taking place on stage, nourishes and superheats created symbols.

These symbols are symbols of full-blown powers held in bond-

18

age until that moment and unusable in real life, exploding in the guise of incredible images giving existence and the freedom of the city to acts naturally opposed to social life.

A real stage play upsets our sensual tranquillity, releases our repressed subconscious, drives us to a kind of potential rebellion (since it retains its full value only if it remains potential), calling for a difficult heroic attitude on the part of the assembled groups.

As soon as the curtain goes up on Ford's *'Tis Pity She's a Whore* to our great surprise we see before us a man launched on a most arrogant defense of incest, exerting all his youthful, conscious strength both in proclaiming and justifying it.

He does not hesitate or waver for one instant, thereby demonstrating just how little all the barriers mean that might be set up against him. He is heroically guilty, boldly, openly heroic. Everything drives him in this direction, inflames him, there is no heaven and no earth for him, only the strength of his tumultuous passion, and Annabella's unsubmissive love does not fall short of his.

"I weep", she says, "not with remorse, but for fear I shall not be able to satisfy my passion." They are both falsifiers, hypocrites and liars for the sake of their superhuman passion obstructed, persecuted by the law, but which they place above the law.

Revenge for revenge, crime for crime. While we believed them threatened, hunted, lost and we were ready to feel pity for them as victims, they show themselves ready to trade blow for blow with fate and threat for threat.

We follow them from one demand to the other, from one excess to the next. Annabella is caught, convicted of adultery and incest, she is trampled upon, insulted, dragged along by the hair but to our great astonishment instead of trying to make excuses she provokes her executioner even more and sings out in a kind of stubborn heroism. This is final rebellion, exemplary love without respite, making the audience gasp with anxiety in case anything should ever end it.

19

If one is looking for an example of total freedom in rebellion, Ford's *'Tis Pity* offers us this poetic example coupled with a picture of ultimate danger.

And just when we think we have reached a climax of horror and bloodshed, of flaunted laws, in short poetry consecrating rebellion, we are obliged to continue in a vortex nothing can stop.

At the end we tell ourselves there must be retribution and death for such boldness and for such an irresistible crime.

Yet it is not so. Giovanni, the lover, inspired by a great impassioned poet, places himself above retribution and crime by a kind of indescribably passionate crime, places himself above threats, above horror by an even greater horror that baffles both law and morals and those who dare to set themselves up as judges.

A clever trap is laid; orders are given for a great banquet where henchmen and hired assassins hide among the guests, ready to pounce on him at the first sign. But this lost, hunted hero inspired by love, will not allow anyone to judge that love.

He seems to say, you want my love's flesh and blood but I mean to hurl it in your face, I intend to splatter you with the blood of a love whose level you could never attain.

And he kills his beloved and rips out her heart as if to eat his fill of it in the midst of that feast where the guests had hoped to devour him themselves.

He kills his rival before his execution, his sister's husband who had dared to come between himself and his mistress, slaying him in a final duel which then appears as his own death throes.

Like the plague, theatre is a powerful appeal through illustration to those powers which return the mind to the origins of its inner struggles. And we clearly sense Ford's passionate example is only a symbol for a much greater and absolutely fundamental task.

The terrifying apparition of Evil produced in unalloyed form at the Eleusian Mysteries being truly revealed, corresponded to the

20

darker moments in certain ancient tragedies which all theatre must rediscover.

If fundamental theatre is like the plague, this is not because it is contagious, but because like the plague it is a revelation, urging forward the exteriorisation of a latent undercurrent of cruelty through which all the perversity of which the mind is capable, whether in a person or a nation, becomes localised.

Just like the plague there is an evil time, the victory of dark powers, a higher power nourishing them until they have died out.

In theatre, as in the plague, there is a kind of strange sun, an unusually bright light by which the difficult, even the impossible suddenly appears to be our natural medium. And Ford's *'Tis Pity She's a Whore* is lit by the brilliance of that strange sun just as is all worthwhile theatre. It resembles the plague's freedom where, step by step, stage by stage, the victim's character swells out, where the survivors gradually become imposing, superhuman beings.

Now one may say all true freedom is dark, infallibly identified with sexual freedom, also dark, without knowing exactly why. For the Platonic Eros, the genetic meaning of a free life, disappeared long ago beneath the turbid surface of the *Libido* we associate with everything sullied, despicable and ignominious in being alive, to rush headlong with our customary, impure vitality, with constantly renewed strength, in the direction of life.

Thus all great Myths are dark and one cannot imagine all the great Fables aside from a mood of slaughter, torture and bloodshed, telling the masses about the original division of the sexes and the slaughter of essences that came with creation.

Theatre, like the plague, is made in the image of this slaughter, this essential division. It unravels conflicts, liberates powers, releases potential and if these and the powers are dark, this is not the fault of the plague or theatre, but life.

We do not see that life as it stands and as it has been made offers us much cause for exaltation. It seems as though a colossal abcess, ethical as much as social, is drained by the plague. And like the plague, theatre is collectively made to drain abcesses.

It may be true that the poison of theatre, when injected in the body of society, destroys it as St. Augustine asserted, but it does so as a plague, a revenging scourge, a redeeming epidemic when credulous ages were convinced they saw God's hand in it, while it was nothing more than a natural law applied, where all gestures were offset by another gesture, every action by a reaction.

Like the plague, theatre is a crisis resolved either by death or cure. The plague is a superior disease because it is an absolute crisis after which there is nothing left except death or drastic purification. In the same way, theatre is a disease because it is a final balance that cannot be obtained without destruction. It urges the mind on to delirium which intensifies its energy. And finally from a human view point we can see that theatre action is as beneficial as the plague, impelling us to see ourselves as we are, making the masks fall and divulging our world's lies, aimlessness, meanness, and even two-facedness. It shakes off stifling material dullness which even overcomes the senses' clearest testimony, and collectively reveals their dark powers and hidden strength to men, urging them to take a nobler, more heroic stand in the face of destiny than they would have assumed without it.

And the question we must now ask ourselves is to know whether in this world that is slipping away, committing suicide without realising it, a nucleus of men can be found to impress this higher idea of theatre on the world, to bring back to all of us a natural, occult equivalent of the dogma we no longer believe.

PRODUCTION AND METAPHYSICS

There is a work by a Primitive painter in the Louvre, whether known or unknown I cannot say, who will never represent a major school in art history. The artist's name is Lucas van Leyden and to my mind he invalidates the four or five hundred years of painting coming after him, rendering them useless. The painting in question is entitled *Lot and his Daughters,* a biblical subject in the style of the period. The Middle Ages certainly did not interpret the Bible as we do today and this painting is a strange example of the mystical inferences which can be deduced from it. In any event, its pathos is noticeable even from a distance, since it affects the mind by a kind of striking visual harmony, intensely active in the whole work yet caught at a glance. Even before we have made out the subject, we get the feeling something important is happening and it seems the ear is as affected by it as the eye. A tremendously important mental drama appears accumulated there, like a sudden cloud formation which the wind or some more immediate fate has blown there to assess their thunderbolts.

And in fact, in the painting the sky is dark and overcast, but even before we can make out that this drama originated in the heavens, took place in the heavens, the strange colouring and jumble of forms, the impression emanating from it at a distance, all foretells a kind of natural drama and I defy any other artist of the Golden

23

Ages to offer us anything like it.

A tent is pitched on the shore, in front of which Lot is seated, wearing a breastplate and sporting a fine red beard, watching his daughters parade before him as if he were a guest at a prostitutes banquet.

And in fact they strut about, some mothers, others Amazons, combing their hair or fencing, as if they had never had any other object than to please their father, to serve as his creatures or playthings. Here we see the deeply incestuous nature of this old subject which the artist has developed in sexual imagery, a proof that he has fully understood all its deep sexuality in a modern way, that is to say as we would understand it ourselves. A proof that its deeply sexual but poetic nature did not escape him any more than it did us.

On the left of the painting, slightly in the background, a black tower rises to fantastic heights, its base supported by a network of rocks and plants, twisting roads marked by milestones, with houses dotted here and there. And by an apt perspective effect, one of these paths which had been threading its way through the maze stands out at a given spot, crosses a bridge, is finally caught in a shaft of that storm lighting spilling out between the clouds, in which the region is fitfully bathed. In the background, the sea is very high besides being extraordinarily calm considering the fiery web seething in one corner of the sky.

Sometimes, when we are watching exploding fireworks, some details of the landscape stand out against the darkness in the ghostly light, in the nocturnal gunfire of shooting stars, sky rockets and Roman candles; trees, tower, mountains and houses appear in relief before our eyes, their colour and appearance forever remaining associated in our minds with a notion of ear-splitting noise. There is no better way of conveying how the various aspects of the landscape conform to this fire revealed in the sky, than by saying that although they possess their own colour, in spite of everything, they remain related to it like muted echoes, like living points of reference born within it, put there to allow it to exert its full destructive power.

Besides, there is something horribly forceful and disturbing about the way the painter depicts this fire, like active, changing features in a set expression. It makes little difference how this effect is achieved, it is real. One has only to see the painting to be convinced of it.

In any case, this fire, which no one will deny gives one the impression of an evil intellect emanating from it, by its very violence mentally serves to counterbalance the heavy material solidity of the remainder.

To the right, on the same perspective level as the Black Tower, a narrow spit of land surrounded by a ruined monastery juts out between the heavens and high seas.

This spit of land, however near it may appear to the shore where Lot's tent is pitched, still leaves room for a vast gulf where an unprecedented maritime disaster seems to have taken place. Ships broken in two but not yet sunk are propped up on the sea as if on crutches, while the water round about them is full of their uprooted masts and broken spars.

It is hard to say why such an impression of absolute disaster emanates from the sight of one or two shipwrecked vessels.

It seems as though the painter knew certain secrets about linear proportion and how to make it affect the mind directly like a physical reagent. In any case this impression of intellect spread abroad in outdoor nature, especially the manner of portraying it, is apparent in several other details on the canvas, such as the bridge standing out against the sea, high as an eight-story house with people filing across it like Ideas in Plato's cave.

It would be untrue to claim that the thoughts emerging from this painting are clear. At all events they are of a grandeur to which we have become totally unaccustomed during the last few centuries by painting that was merely painting.

In addition, Lot and his daughters suggest an idea of sexuality

25

and reproduction and Lot seems placed there like a drone, to take improper advantage of his daughters.

This is almost the only social idea in the picture.

All the other ideas are metaphysical. I am sorry to have to use that word, but that is what they are called. And I might even say their poetic greatness, their tangible effect on us arises from the fact that they are metaphysical, that their mental profundity cannot be separated from the painting's formal, external symmetry.

Furthermore there is an idea of change in the different land-scape details and the way they are painted, their levels annulling or corresponding to one another, lead us into the mind in painting the same way as in music.

There is another idea about Fate, revealed not so much by the appearance of that sudden fire as by the solemn way in which all forms are arranged or disarranged beneath it, some as if bent beneath a gust of irresistible panic, the others motionless, almost ironic, all obeying a powerful intelligent consistency, seemingly nature's mind externalised.

There are also ideas on Chaos, the Marvellous and Balance. There are even one or two on the impotence of Words, this sup-remely anarchic, material painting seeming to establish their futility.

In any event I must say this painting is what theatre ought to be, if only it knew how to speak its own language.

And I ask this question:

How can it be that in the theatre, at least theatre such as we know it in Europe, or rather in the West, everything specifically theatrical, that is to say everything which cannot be expressed in words or if you prefer, everything that is not contained in dialogue (dialogue itself viewed as a function of sound amplification on stage and the *requirements* of that sound) has been left in the background?

Besides, how can it be that Western theatre (I say Western theatre as luckily there are others such as Oriental theatre, which have known how to keep theatre concepts intact, whereas in the West this idea – just like all others – has been *debased*), how is it Western theatre cannot conceive of theatre under any other aspect than dialogue form?

Dialogue – something written and spoken – does not specifically belong to the stage but to books. The proof is that there is a special section in literary history textbooks on drama as a subordinate branch in the history of spoken language.

I maintain the stage is a tangible, physical place that needs to be filled and it ought to be allowed to speak its own concrete language.

I maintain that this physical language, aimed at the senses and independent of speech, must first satisfy the senses. There must be poetry for the senses just as there is for speech, but this physical, tangible language I am referring to is really only theatrical in as far as the thoughts it expresses escape spoken language.

You might ask what these thoughts are that words cannot express, and which would find a more fitting, ideal expression than words in a physical, tangible stage language?

I will answer this question later.

The most urgent thing seems to me to decide what this physical language is composed of, this solid, material language by which theatre can be distinguished from words.

It is composed of everything filling the stage, everything that can be shown and materially expressed on stage, intended first of all to appeal to the senses, instead of being addressed primarily to the mind, like spoken language. (I am well aware words also have their own sound potential, different ways of being projected into space, called *inflexion*. Besides one could say a great deal about the tangible value of inflexions in theatre, about the faculty words also have of creating their own music according to the way they are pronounced, distinct from their actual meaning and even running counter to that meaning – to create an undercurrent of impressions, connections and affinities beneath language. But this

27

theatrical way of looking at language is already a subordinate *aspect* to the dramatist and one to which he no longer pays attention, especially today, in creating his plays. Well, let it go at that.)

This language created for the senses must first take care to satisfy the senses. This would not prevent it later amplifying its full mental effect on all possible levels and along all lines. It would also permit spatial poetry to take the place of language poetry and to be resolved in the exact field of whatever does not properly apply to words.

In order to understand what I have said better, doubtless a few examples of this spatial poetry would be desirable, able as it is to give birth to those kinds of substantial imagery, the equivalent of word imagery. Examples will be found below.

This difficult, complex poetry assumes many guises; first of all it assumes those expressive means usable on stage* such as music, dance, plastic art, mimicry, mime, gesture, voice inflexion, architecture, lighting and decor.

Each of these means has its own specific poetry as well as a kind of ironic poetry arising from the way it combines with other expressive means. It is easy to see the result of these combinations, their interaction and mutual subversion.

I will return below to the subject of this poetry which can only be fully effective if it is tangible, that is to say if it objectively produces something owing to its *active* presence on stage – if, as in the Balinese theatre, a sound corresponds to a certain gesture and instead of acting as decor accompanying thought, makes it develop, guiding it, destroying it or decisively changing it, etc.

One form of this spatial poetry – beyond any brought about by an arrangement of lines, forms, colours, and objects in their natural

---

* In as far as they show themselves able to profit by the direct physical potential offered by the stage, to replace the set forms of the art with living, threatening forms, through which the meaning of ancient ceremonial magic can find fresh reality on a theatrical level. In as far as they accede to what one might call the *physical temptation* of the stage.

state, such as are found in all the arts – belongs to sign language. And I hope I may mention that other aspect of pure theatre language that escapes words, that sign, gesture and posture language with its own ideographic values such as they exist in some undebased mime plays.

By "undebased mime plays" I mean straightforward mime where gestures, instead of standing for words or sentences as in European mime (barely fifty years old) where they are merely a distortion of the silent parts in Italian comedy, stand for ideas, attitudes of mind, aspects of nature in a tangible, potent way, that is to say by always evoking natural things or details, like that Oriental language portraying night by a tree on which a bird that has already closed one eye, is beginning to close the other. And another abstract idea or attitude of mind could be portrayed by some of the innumerable symbols in Scripture, such as the eye of the needle through which the camel cannot pass.

We can see these signs form true hieroglyphics where man, in as far as he contributes to making them, is only one form like any other, to which he nevertheless adds particular prestige because of his duality.

This language conjures up intense images of natural or mental poetry in the mind and gives us a good idea of what spatial poetry, if free from spoken language, could become in the theatre.

Whatever the position of this language and poetry may be, I have noticed that in our theatre, which exists under the exclusive dictatorship of words, this language of symbols and mimicry, this silent mime-play, these attitudes, and spatial gestures, this objective inflexion, in short everything I look on as specifically theatrical in theatre, all these elements when they exist outside the script, are generally considered the lowest part of theatre, are casually called "craft" and are associated with what is known as staging or "production". We are lucky when the word staging is not just tagged on to the idea of external artistic lavishness solely connected with costume, lighting and decor.

29

Against this viewpoint, which seems to me completely Western or rather Latin, that is, pig-headed, I might even say that in as much as this language starts on stage, drawing its effectiveness from its spontaneous creation on stage, in as much as it exerts itself directly on stage without passing through words (and why could we not envisage a play composed right on stage, produced on stage) – staging is theatre far more than a written, spoken play. No doubt I will be asked what is specifically Latin about this view which is opposed to mime. What is Latin is the need to use words to express obvious ideas. For me obvious ideas, in theatre as in all else, are dead and finished.

The idea of a play built right on stage, encountering production and performance obstacles, demands the discovery of active language, both active and anarchic, where the usual limits of feelings and words are transcended.

In any event, and I hasten to say so at once, theatre which submits staging and production, that is to say everything about it that is specifically theatrical, to the lines, is mad, crazy, perverted, rhetorical, philistine, antipoetic and Positivist, – that is to say, Western theatre.

Furthermore, I am well aware that a language of gestures and postures, dance and music is less able to define a character, to narrate man's thoughts, to explain conscious states clearly and exactly, than spoken language. But whoever said theatre was made to define a character, to resolve conflicts of a human, emotional order, of a present-day, psychological nature such as those which monopolise current theatre?

Given theatre as we see it here, one would imagine there was nothing more to know than whether we will have a good fuck, whether we will go to war or be cowardly enough to sue for peace, how we will put up with our petty moral anxieties, whether we will become conscious of our "complexes" (in scientific language) or whether our "complexes" will silence us. Moreover, rarely does the debate rise to a social level or do we question our social or ethical system. Our theatre never goes so far as to ask itself whether by chance this social or ethical system is iniquitous or not.

Now to my mind the present state of society is iniquitous and ought to be destroyed. If it is theatre's role to be concerned with it, it is even more a matter for machine-guns. Our theatre is not even able to ask this question in as effective and incendiary a manner as is needed, and even if it did ask it, it would still be far from its intended purpose which is higher and even more mysterious.

All the topics detailed above stink of mankind, of materialistic, temporary mankind, I might even say *carrion-man*. These personal worries disgust me, utterly disgust me as does just about all current theatre, which is as human as it is antipoetic and, except for three or four plays, seems to me to stink of decadence and pus.

Current theatre is in decline because on the one hand it has lost any feeling for seriousness, and on the other for laughter. Because it has broken away from solemnity, from direct, harmful effectiveness – in a word, from Danger.

For it has lost any true sense of humour, and laughter's physical, anarchic, dissolving power.

Because it has broken away from the profoundly anarchic spirit at the basis of all poetry.

One must admit that everything in the purpose of an object, the meaning or use of a natural form, is a matter of convention.

When nature gave a tree the shape of a tree, it could just as well have given it the shape of an animal or a hill and we would have thought *tree* before animal or hill and the trick would have been played.

We all agree a beautiful woman has a pleasing voice. Yet if from when the world began we had heard all beautiful women call us by snorting through their trunks and greet us by trumpeting, we would ever after have associated the idea of trumpeting with the idea of a beautiful woman and a part of our inner vision of the world would have been radically changed.

Thus we can understand poetry is anarchic in as much as it

questions all object relationships or those between meaning and form. It is also anarchic to the extent its occurrence is the result of disturbances leading us nearer to chaos.

I will give no further examples. One could go on for ever, not only with humorous ones such as those I have just used.

Theatrically, this inversion of forms, these altered meanings, could become the essential element of this humorous spatial poetry, staging's exclusive province.

In one of the Marx Brothers' films a man, thinking he is about to take a woman in his arms, ends up with a cow which moos. And through a combination of circumstances too long to relate, at that moment that same moo assumes an intellectual dignity equal to a woman's cry.

If such a situation is possible in films, it is no less possible in theatre as it stands, and it would take very little; for example the cow might be replaced by an animated puppet, a kind of monster gifted with speech, or a man disguised as an animal – to rediscover the secret of the objective poetry underlying all humour, which theatre has given up, leaving it for Music-Hall, while the cinema later turned it to good account.

I mentioned danger in a preceding paragraph. Now it seems to me the best way of producing this concept of danger on stage is by the objective unforeseen, not unforeseen in situations but in things, the sudden inopportune passing from a mental image to a true image. For example a man cursing suddenly sees the image of his curse realistically materialised before him (provided, I might add, this image was not utterly pointless, but engenders in turn other imagery of the same mental spirit).

Another example would be to have a fabricated being appear, made of wood and cloth, completely invented, resembling nothing, yet disturbing in nature, able to reintroduce on stage the slightest intimation of the great metaphysical fear underlying all ancient theatre.

The Balinese with their imaginary dragon, like all Orientals,

32

have not lost the sense of this mysterious fear, since they know it is one of the most stirring and indeed essential elements in theatre when the latter is restored to its proper level.

For whether we like it or not, true poetry is metaphysical and I might even say it is its metaphysical scope, its degree of metaphysical effectiveness, which gives it its proper value.

This is the second or third time I have mentioned metaphysics. I also mentioned dead ideas above while speaking about psychology and I expect many people will be tempted to tell me that if there is one inhuman idea on earth, one ineffective, dead idea which means very little even to the mind, it is metaphysics.

As René Guénon said, this is due "to our purely Western manner, our anti-poetic, truncated way of regarding first principles, (apart from the forceful, massive state of mind corresponding to them)."

In Oriental theatre with its metaphysical inclinations, as against Western theatre and its psychological inclinations, this whole complex of gestures, signs, postures and sound which make up a stage production language, this language which develops all its physical and poetic effects on all conscious levels and in all senses, must lead to thought adopting deep attitudes which might be called *active metaphysics*.

I will return to this later. For the moment let us go back to theatre as we know it.

I attended a discussion on theatre a few days ago where I saw some of those creepy men, otherwise known as playwrights, come and explain to me how to insinuate a play into a producer's favour, like those men in history who *introduced* poison into their rival's ears. I believe the matter under discussion was settling the direction theatre must take, in other words its future destiny.

Nothing was settled and at no time was there any question of theatre's true fate, that is to say what, by nature and definition, theatre is destined to represent, nor those means at its command to do so. On the contrary, theatre seemed to me like a kind of frozen

33

world, with players frozen in gestures that were no longer of any use to them, brittle inflexions overheard already falling to pieces, with music reduced to kinds of ciphers whose signs were beginning to fade, and kinds of luminous explosions, themselves solidified and corresponding to the traces of moves – and all about an incredible fluttering of men in black suits busy arguing over receipts by the entrance to a white-hot box office. As if theatre organisation were henceforth reduced to everything peripheral and theatre was reduced to everything that is not theatre, while its pervading tone stinks to high heaven to people of taste.

To my mind theatre merges with production potential when the most extreme poetic results are derived from it, and theatre's production potential is wholly related to staging viewed as a language of movement in space.

Now to derive the furthest poetic consequences from means of production is to make metaphysics out of them and I do not believe anyone could argue with that way of looking at the problem.

It seems to me that to make metaphysics out of language, gestures, postures, decor and music is, from a theatrical point of view, to regard it in relation to all the ways it can have of agreeing with time and movement.

To give objective examples of the poetry resulting from the various ways gesture, sound or inflexion supports itself with more or less insistence on such and such a spatial area at such and such a moment, would appear to me as difficult as to communicate the feeling of the special quality of a sound in words, or the intensity and nature of physical pain. It all depends on production and can only be determined on stage.

Here and now I ought to review all the means of expression open to theatre (or staging, which in the system I have just expanded, is merged with it). But that would entail too much and I will select only one or two examples.

First, on spoken language.

34

To make metaphysics out of spoken language is to make language convey what it does not normally convey. That is to use it in a new, exceptional and unusual way, to give it its full, physical shock potential, to split it up and distribute it actively in space, to treat inflexions in a completely tangible manner and restore their shattering power and really to manifest something; to turn against language and its basely utilitarian, one might almost say alimentary, sources, against its origins as a hunted beast, and finally to consider language in the form of *Incantation*.

This whole active, poetic way of visualising stage expression leads us to turn away from present-day theatre's human, psychological meaning and to rediscover a religious, mystical meaning our theatre has forgotten.

Besides, if one has only to say words like *religious* and *mystic* to be taken for a sexton or a profoundly illiterate bonze only fit for rattling prayer wheels outside a Buddhist temple, this is a simple judgement on our incapacity to draw all the inferences from words and our profound ignorance of the spirit of synthesis and analogy.

It may also mean that we have reached the point where we have lost all contact with true theatre, since we restrict it to the field of whatever everyday thought can achieve, to the known or unknown field of consciousness – and if theatrically we turn to the subconscious it is merely to steal what it may have been able to collect (or hide) in the way of accessible pedestrian experiences.

Let it be further said that one of the reasons for the physical effectiveness on the mind, the direct, active power of the images in certain Oriental theatre productions such as those by the Balinese theatre, is that theatre rests on age old traditions, having kept the secret use of gestures, inflexions and harmony intact, in relation to the senses and on all possible levels – this does not condemn Oriental theatre but censures us and with us the state we live in, which must be destroyed so we may apply ourselves to eliminating it vindictively in every sphere where it hinders the free application of thought.

ON THE BALINESE THEATRE

The first Balinese Theatre show derived from dance, singing, mime and music – but extraordinarily little from psychological theatre such as we understand it in Europe, re-establishing theatre from a hallucinatory and fearful aspect, on a purely independent, creative level.

It is most remarkable that the first of the short plays in this spectacle shows us a father admonishing his custom-flouting daughter and begins with the entrance of ghosts. Or rather, the male and female characters who are going to enact the unfolding of this stock dramatic theme first appear as characters in ghostly form, and are seen in the guise of an illusion proper to all dramatic characters, before allowing any development in the situations of this kind of figurative sketch. Anyway, the situations only serve as a pretext in this case and the play does not develop through the emotions but through states of mind, themselves stilted and epitomised in gestures – outlines. In short the Balinese produce the idea of pure theatre with the greatest exactness, where everything in concept and production is valued and only exists through the degree of its objectification *on stage*. They triumphantly demonstrate the absolute superiority of the producer whose creative ability *does away with words*. The themes are very general, indefinite and abstract. Only a complex expansion of stage artifice

36

brings them to life, imposing on our minds something like the idea of a metaphysics coined from a new usage of gestures and speech.

In fact the strange thing about all these gestures, these angular, sudden, jerky postures, these syncopated inflexions formed at the back of the throat, these musical phrases cut short, the sharded flights, rustling branches, hollow drum sounds, robot creaking, animated puppets dancing, is the feeling of a new bodily language no longer based on words but on signs which emerges through the maze of gestures, postures, airborne cries, through their gyrations and turns, leaving not even the smallest area of stage space unused. Those actors with their asymmetrical robes looking like moving hieroglyphs; not just the shape of their gowns, shifting the axis of the human figure, but creating a kind of second symbolic clothing standing beside the uniforms of those warriors entranced and perpetually at war, thus inspiring intellectual ideas or merely connecting all the criss-crossing of these lines with all the criss-crossing of spatial perspective. These mental signs have an exact meaning that only strikes one intuitively, but violently enough to make any translations into logical, discursive language useless. And for lovers of out-and-out realism, who might grow tired of the constant allusions to hidden, out of the way attitudes of mind, there is still the double's nobly realistic acting, terrified as he is by apparitions from the Other World. There is a delineation of fear valid for all latitudes in this double who, by his trembling, childish yelping and heels striking the ground in time with the very automatism of the unleashed subconscious, hides behind his own reality, showing us that in human as well as in superhuman fields, Orientals are more than a match for us in matters of realism.

The Balinese, with gestures and a variety of mime to suit all occasions in life, reinstate the superior value of theatre conventions, demonstrate the effectiveness and greater active value of a certain number of well-learnt and above all masterfully applied conventions. One of the reasons for our delight in this faultless show lies precisely in the use these actors make of an exact amount of assured gesture, tried and tested mime coming in at an appointed place, but particularly in the mental clothing, in the deep shaded study which governs the formulation of the expressive interplay of these effective signs, giving us the impression their effectiveness has not become weakened over the centuries. That mechanical eye-rolling, those pouting lips, the use of twitching muscles producing studiously calculated effects which prevent any resorting to spontaneous improvisation, those heads moving horizontally seem-ing to slide from one shoulder to the other as if on rollers, all that corresponds to direct psychological needs as well as to a kind of mental construction made up of gestures, mime, the evocative power of rhythm, the musical quality of physical movement, the comparable, wonderfully fused harmony of a note. This may shock our European sense of stage freedom and spontaneous inspiration, but let no one say their precision makes for sterility or monotony. We get a marvellous feeling of richness, fantasy and bounteous lavishness emanating from this show regulated with a maddeningly conscious attention to detail. And the most impulsive correlations constantly fuse sight with sound, intellect with sensibility, a character's gestures with the evocation of a plant's movements through the aid of an instrumental cry. The sighs of a wind instru-ment prolong the vibrations of vocal cords so identically we do not know whether the voice itself is held, or the senses which first assi-milated that voice. Those rippling joints, the musical angle the arm makes with a forearm, a falling foot, an arching knee, fingers that seem to come loose from the hand, all this is like a constant play of mirrors where human limbs seem to echo one another, harmonious orchestral notes and the whisper of wind instruments, conjure up the idea of a passionate aviary where the actors themselves are the fluttering wings. Our theatre has never grasped this gestured metaphysics nor known how to make use of music for direct, concrete, dramatic purposes, our purely verbal theatre unaware of the sum total of theatre, of everything that exists spatially on the boards or is measured and circumscribed in space, having spatial

38

density (moves, forms, colours, vibrations, postures, shouts) could learn a lesson in spirituality from the Balinese theatre with regard to the indeterminable, to dependence on the mind's suggestive power. This purely popular, non-religious theatre gives us an extraordinary idea of a nation's intellectual level, which takes the struggle of a soul as prey to the spectres and phantoms of the Other World to be the basis for its civic festivals. For the last part of the show certainly deals with purely inner conflicts. And in passing we ought to note the extent of theatrical magnificence the Balinese have been able to impart to it. The sense of the stage's plastic requirements are seen to be equalled only by their knowledge of physical fear and how to unleash it. And there is a striking similarity between the truly terrifying look of their devil, probably of Tibetan origin, and a certain puppet with leafy green nails, its hands distended with white gelatine, the finest ornament of one of the first plays of the Alfred Jarry Theatre.

*

This show is more than we can approach head on, bombarding us as it does with an overabundance of impressions each one more splendid than the last, but in a language to which we no longer seem to hold the key, and a kind of annoyance is caused by being unable to run it to earth or rediscover the thread, to turn one's ear closer to the instrument to hear it better, just one more charm to add to the show's credit. And by language I do not mean an idiom we fail to catch at first hearing, but precisely that kind of theatrical language foreign to every *spoken language*, where it seems a tremendous stage experience is recaptured, beside which our exclusively dialogue productions seem like so much stammering.

In fact, the most striking thing about this show – so well-contrived to baffle our Western concept of theatre that many may well deny it any dramatic qualities whereas it is the finest demonstration of pure theatre we have ever been privileged to see here – what is striking and disturbing about it for us as Europeans is the

39

wonderful intelligence seeming to spark through the compact texture of gestures, in the infinitely varied voice inflexions, in that tempest of sound resounding as if from a vast, dripping rain forest, and in the equally sonorous interlacing moves. There is no transition from a gesture to a cry or a sound; everything is connected as if through strange channels penetrating right through the mind!

There is a horde of ritual gestures in it to which we have no key, seeming to obey a very precise, musical indication, with something added that does not usually belong to music and seems to be aimed at encircling thought, hounding it down, leading it into a sure, labyrinthine system. In fact everything in this theatre is assessed with loving, unerring attention to detail. Nothing is left either to chance or individual initiative. It is a kind of sublime dance where the dancers are actors first and foremost.

We see them repeatedly carry out a kind of reanimation at a measured tread. Just as they appear to be lost in a hopelessly intricate maze of beats and we feel they are about to fall prey to confusion, they have their own way of regaining their balance, a peculiar arching, leg twisting stance which gives the impression of a wet cloth about to be wrung to music – suddenly the floating rhythm ends, the beat becomes clear on three final steps, inevitably bringing them back to centre stage.

Everything is just as ordered and just as impersonal with them. Not one rippling muscle, not one rolling eye does not seem to belong to a kind of deliberate accuracy directing everything, through which everything happens. The odd thing is that in this systematic depersonalisation, in the purely muscular facial expressions, like feature masks, everything produces, conveys the utmost effect.

We are seized with a kind of terror when we think of these mechanical beings whose happiness and pain seem not to be their own, but to obey tried and tested rituals as if governed by higher intellects. In the last analysis, this impression of a higher, controlled life is what strikes us most about this show, like a profane ritual. It has the solemnity of a holy ritual – the hieratic costumes give each actor a kind of dual body, dual limbs – and in his costume, the stiff stilted artist seems merely his own effigy. Beside the booming, pounding musical rhythm – there is a sustained hesitating fragile music which seems to grind the most precious metals, where springs of water bubble up as in a state of nature, where columns of insects march through the plants, where the sound of light itself appears to have been picked up, where the sounds of deep solitudes seem distilled into crystal swarms.

Furthermore, all these sounds are linked to movements, they are like the natural conclusion of gestures with the same attributes. All this with such a feeling of musical similarity, the mind is at last obliged to confuse them, attributing the sound qualities of the orchestra to the artist's hinged gesticulation – and vice versa.

An inhuman, sacred, miraculously revealing impression emanates from the exquisite beauty of the women's headdress, a series of radiant tiers made up of arrangements of multi-coloured feathers, from pearls so lovely their colouring, their variegation seems so justly to have been *revealed*, the crests tremble rhythmically, seeming *consciously* to answer the trembling bodies. There are also the other headdresses of a priestly appearance, in tiara form, topped with egret crests and tufts of stiff flowers in pairs of contrasting, strangely harmonised colours.

This throbbing ensemble full of rockets, flights, canals, detours in all the directions of our inner and outer perception, creates theatre as a sovereign idea such as it has been preserved for us through the ages, to teach us what it ought never to have stopped being. And this impression is increased by the fact that this show – popular out there it seems, and profane – is like the daily bread of these people's artistic feelings.

Aside from this show's stupendous precision, the thing which seems to surprise and astonish us the most is this *revealing aspect of matter*, suddenly seeming to disperse in signs, to teach us the metaphysical identity of abstract and concrete and to teach it to us in *lasting gestures*. For though we are familiar with its realistic

41

aspect, here it is raised to the *nth* power and absolutely stylised.

*

All creativity stems from the stage in this drama, finding its expression and even its sources in a secret psychic impulse, speech prior to words.

*

This theatre does away with the playwright to the advantage of what in Western theatre jargon we call the producer. But the latter becomes a kind of organiser of magic, a master of holy ceremonies. And the material on which he works, the subjects he makes thrilling are not his own but descend from the gods. They seem to stem from primal unions in Nature promoted by a double Spirit.

What he sets in motion is MANIFEST.

A kind of ancient Natural Philosophy, from which the mind has never been separated.

*

There is something about a spectacle like the Balinese Theatre which does away with entertainment, that aspect of useless artificiality, an evening's amusement so typical of our own theatre. Its productions are hewn out of matter itself before our eyes, in real life itself. There is something of a religious ritual ceremony about them, in the sense that they eradicate any idea of pretence, a ridiculous imitation of real life, from the spectator's mind. This involved gesticulation we see has a goal, an immediate goal towards which it aims by effective means, and we are able to experience its direct effectiveness. The thought it aims at, the states of mind it attempts to create, the mystical discoveries it offers are motivated and reached without delay or periphrasis. It all seems like an exorcism to make our devils FLOW.

42

This theatre vibrates with instinctive things but brought to that lucid, intelligent, malleable point where they seem physically to supply us with some of the mind's most secret perceptions.

We might say the subjects presented begin on stage. They have reached such a point of objective materialisation we could not imagine them, however much one might try, outside this compact panorama, the enclosed, confined world of the stage.

This show gives us a wonderful compound of pure stage imagery and a whole new language seems to have been invented in order to make it understood. The actors and costumes form true, living, moving hieroglyphs. And these three-dimensional hieroglyphics are in turn embellished with a certain number of gestures, strange signs matching some dark prodigious reality we have repressed once and for all here in the West.

There is something of the state of mind of a magic act in this intensive liberation of signs, at first held back, then abruptly launched into the air.

Confused seething, full of recognisable particles at times strangely orderly, sparkles in the effervescence of these painted rhythms, where the fermata constantly play and are interposed like calculated silences.

But no one in the West has ever tried to bring this concept of pure theatre to life since we regard it as merely theoretical, whereas the Balinese Theatre offers us an outstanding production that suppresses any likelihood of recourse to words to clarify the most abstract subjects; it has invented a language of gestures to be spatially developed, but having no meaning outside it.

The stage is used in all its dimensions, one might even say on all possible levels. For besides a keen sense of plastic beauty, these gestures are always ultimately aimed at the clarification of a state of mind or mental problem.

At least that is how it appears to us.

No point in space, and at the same time no possible intimations are wasted. And there is something like a philosophical feeling of the power nature has to rush suddenly headlong into chaos.

*

In the Balinese Theatre one senses a state prior to language, able to select its own language; music, gestures, moves and words.

*

We can be sure this aspect of pure theatre, this natural philosophy of total gesture, an idea in itself, transforming the mind's persuasions in order to be discerned through the fibrous maze and tangle of matter, gives us a new idea of whatever properly belongs to the field of form and visible matter. Anyone who succeeds in imparting a mystical meaning to the simple outline of a gown, not simply content with placing man beside his Double, but ascribing to each costumed person their costumed double – those who run these phantasmal clothes, these second clothes, through with a sword, giving them the look of huge butterflies pinned in the air, these people have a far more inborn sense than us of nature's total, occult symbolism, teaching us a lesson which we can be only too sure our theatre technicians would be incapable of using.

*

The intellectual space, psychic interplay and silence solidified by thought existing between the parts of a written sentence, are drawn on stage between the parts, areas and sight-lines of a certain number of shouts, colours and moves.

*

In the Balinese Theatre productions the mind certainly gets the feeling that concepts clashed with gestures first, establishing themselves among a whole ferment of sight and sound imagery, thoughts as it were in a pure state. To sum it up more distinctly, something like a musical condition must have existed to produce

44

this staging, where everything that is imagined by the mind is only an excuse, a virtuality whose double produced this intense scenic poetry, this many-hued spatial language.

*

This constantly mirrored interplay, passing from a colour to a gesture, from cries to movements, endlessly leads us along rough paths that are difficult for the mind, pitching us into that uncertainty, that indescribably anxious state most suited to poetry.

A kind of awful fixation emanates from the strange rippling of flying hands, like insects in the green night, an inexhaustible mental rationalisation as if the mind were perpetually busy getting its bearings within the maze of its own subconscious.

Besides, the things this theatre makes tangible are much less emotional than intellectual, enclosing them as it does within concrete, though almost constantly esoteric, signs.

Thus we are led along intellectual paths towards reconquering the signs of existence.

From this point of view the star dancer's gesture is highly significant, always touching the same spot on his head as he does, as if he wanted to mark the place and existence of some focal mind's eye.

*

Something which is a highly coloured allusion to physical impressions of nature recaptures them on a sensory level, the sound itself being only a nostalgic image of something else, a kind of magic state where feelings have become so sensitive they are suitable for visitation by the mind. Even the imitative harmonies, the sound of a rattle-snake for instance or insect shells splintering against one another, evoke the clearing in a teeming landscape ready to hurl itself into chaos. And those performers dressed in dazzling costumes whose bodies underneath them seemed wrapped in swaddling clothes! There is something umbilical, larval about their movements. At the same time we ought to note the hierogly-phic appearance of the costumes, the horizontal lines extending out beyond the body in all directions. They are like giant insects covered with lines and segments made to unite them with unknown natural perspectives of which they appear as nothing more than its untangented geometry.

These costumes which encircle their abstract sliding walk, the strange criss-crossing of their feet!

Every one of their moves draws a line in space, an unknown meticulous figure of predetermined hermeticism, which an unfore-seen gesture completes.

And the folds of these robes curving above their buttocks, holding them up as if suspended in the air, as if pinned onto the backdrop, prolonging each of their leaps into flight.

Those howls, those rolling eyes, that unceasing abstraction, those sounds of branches, of chopping and log-rolling, all in a vast expanse of sounds flowing out from several outlets at once, all combine to give rise in our minds, to crystallise a new concept, what one might term a concrete concept of the abstract.

It is worth noting that this abstraction, which originates in a wonderful stage construction to return into thought, when it en-counters impressions of the natural world in motion it always grasps them at the point where they penetrate their molecular grouping. That is to say, only a gesture narrowly keeps us from chaos.

*

The last part of the show is divinely anachronistic when com-pared with everything that is dirty, brutish and ignominiously chewed up on the European stage. And I do not know any theatre that would *naturalistically* dare to pin down the horrors of a soul as prey to the ghosts of the Other World in this way.

*

These metaphysicians of natural chaos dance, restoring every

46

iota of sound, each fragmentary perception, as if it were ready to return to its origins, able to wed movement and sound so perfectly it seems the dancers have hollow limbs to make sounds of woodblocks, resounding drums and echoing instruments with their hollow, wooden limbs.

Here we are suddenly in the thick of a metaphysical struggle and the rigid aspect of the body in a trance, tensed by the surging of the cosmic powers attacking it, is admirably expressed in that frenzied dance full of angular stiffness, where we suddenly feel the mind's headlong fall begins.

They seem like substantial waves, dashing their crests into the deep, and rushing from all points of the horizon to hurtle themselves into an infinitesimal portion of a quivering trance – to cover the void of fear.

*

There is something absolute about these spatial constructions, the kind of true physical absolute only Orientals can envisage – for they differ from our European theatre concepts in the sublimity and the considered daring of their aims even more than in the strange perfection of their productions.

Supporters of classifications and divisioning into categories may pretend to see mere dancers in the Balinese Theatre's magnificent performers, dancers entrusted with portraying some great Myth or other whose sublimity makes the level of modern Western theatre unspeakably crude and childish. The truth is that the Balinese Theatre offers and brings us already produced pure dramatic subjects, while the stage setting bestows a concentrated balance on it, a wholly substantiated attraction.

*

All of this is steeped in deep intoxication, restoring the very elements of rapture and in this rapture we rediscover the dry seething and mineral friction of plants, remains and ruined trees frontally illuminated.

All bestiality and animalism are brought down to that dry gesture, striking sounds as the earth splits open, frozen trees, lowing animals.

The dancers' feet, by that gesture of parting their robes, dissolve thoughts and feelings, returning them to their pure state.

And always confronting the head, that Cyclop's eye, the inner mind's eye sought by that right hand.

Miming, mental gestures, accenting, curtailing, settling, dividing and subdividing feelings, soul states and metaphysical ideas.

This quintessant theatre where objects about-face strangely before returning to abstraction.

*

Their gestures fall so exactly on that woody, hollow drum rhythm, accenting it, grasping it in flight so assuredly, on such summits it seems this music accents the very void in their hollow limbs.

*

The women's stratified, lunar eyes.

Those dream-like eyes appearing to engulf us, before which we see ourselves as *ghosts*.

*

Utterly satisfying dance gestures, turning feet mingling with soul states, those tiny flying hands, the dry, precise tapping.

*

We watch mental alchemy creating a gesture out of a state of mind, the dry, naked, linear gestures our acts might have if they sought the absolute.

*

It happens that these mannerisms, this profuse hieratism with its sliding alphabet, its shrieks of creaking stones, branch sounds, where chopping and log rolling fashion a kind of moving audio-visual substantiated murmuring in the air, in space. And after a moment the magical identification has occurred: WE KNOW WE ARE SPEAKING.

Who, after Arjuna's titanic battle with the Dragon dares say all theatre is not on stage, that is to say, beyond situations and words.

For here, the psychological and dramatic situations have gone into the very mime of the fight, a function of the mystical, athletic acting of their bodies, I might even say the undulatory use of the stage, whose gigantic spiral is disclosed step by step.

The warriors enter the mental forest slithering in fear. A great shudder, something like a prodigious magnetic vertigo overcomes them, and we feel inhuman or mineral meteorites hurtling down on them.

The general trembling in their limbs and their rolling eyes signify more than a physical storm or mental concussion. The sensory pulsing of their bristling heads is excruciating at times – and that music behind them which sways and nourishes some unknown space or other where actual stones finally end rolling.

And behind the Warrior, beset by the fearful cosmic storm, stands the Double giving himself airs, given up to the childishness of his schoolboy gibes, who, aroused by the repercussions of the surging gale, moves unaware in the midst of uncomprehended charms.

ORIENTAL AND WESTERN THEATRE

The Balinese Theatre was not a revelation of a verbal but a physical idea of theatre where drama is encompassed within the limits of everything that can happen on stage, independently of a written script. Whereas with us, the lines gain the upper hand and theatre as we understand it finds itself restricted by them. Thus theatre is a branch of literature, a species of vocal language, and even if we admit a difference between the lines spoken on stage and those read by the eyes, even if we confine theatre to what goes on between the cues, we will never succeed in divorcing theatre from the idea of script production.

This notion, the predominance of the lines in theatre, is deeply rooted in us and we view theatre so much as just a physical reflection of the script, that everything in theatre outside the script, not contained within its limits or strictly determined by it, appears to us to be a part of staging, and inferior to the script.

Given the subservience of theatre to the lines, we might ask ourselves whether theatre by any chance possesses a language of its own, or whether it would really be illusory to consider it an independent, autonomous art for the same reasons as music, painting, dance, etc.

In any case if such a language exists it will inevitably be confused with staging viewed:

1. On the one hand as the lines visually, plastically materialised.

2. On the other, as a language expressing everything which can be said or intended on stage distinct from the lines, everything that can be spatially embodied, affected or disrupted by it.

Once we consider this production language as theatre's pure language, we must discover whether it is capable of attaining the same inner object as the words, whether from a theatrical or mental viewpoint it can claim the same intellectual effectiveness as spoken language. In other words we must not ask ourselves whether it can define thought but whether it *makes us think*, and leads the mind to assume deeply effective attitudes from its own point of view.

In short if one questions the intellectual effectiveness of expression through objective forms, of a language using forms, sound and gesture, one is questioning the intellectual effectiveness of art.

Although we have come to credit art with nothing more than a pleasurable relaxing value, confining it to the purely express use of forms, to the compatibility between certain surface relationships, this in no way diminishes its deeply expressive value. But the mental weakness of the West, where man has especially confused art and aesthetics, is to believe one can have painting used only as painting, dancing as a plastic form alone, as if one wanted to cut art off from everything, to sever the links with all the mystical attitudes they might adopt in confrontation with the absolute.

One therefore understands that theatre, in as much as it remains confined within its own language and in correlation with it, must make a break with topicality. It is not aimed at solving social or psychological conflicts, to serve as a battlefield for moral passions, but to express objectively secret truths, to bring out in active gestures those elements of truth hidden under forms in their encounters with Becoming.

To do that, to link theatre with expressive form potential, with everything in the way of gestures, sound, colours, movement, is to return it to its original purpose, to restore it to a religious, metaphysical position, to reconcile it with the universe.

But while one might say words have their own metaphysical power, no one says we cannot think of speech as well as gestures on a universal level. Besides, it is more effective on this level as a dissociatory force exerted on material appearances, as on all states in which the mind feels settled or tends to relax. We can readily answer that this metaphysical way of looking at dialogue is not used in Western theatre since it does not make it an active power springing from the destruction of appearances to reach the mind, but on the contrary uses it as a final degree of thought, lost in being externalised.

In Western theatre, words are solely used to express psychological conflicts peculiar to man and his position in everyday existence. His conflicts are clearly justifiable in spoken words and whether they remain in the psychological field, cr leave it to pass over into the social field, drama will always concern morality owing to the way in which conflicts attack and disrupt character. And this will always remain in a field where words, verbal solutions, retain their advantage. But these moral conflicts, by their very nature, do not need to be resolved on stage. To make speech or verbal expression dominant over the objective expressiveness of gestures and everything on stage spatially affecting the mind through the senses, means turning our backs on the physical requirements of the stage and rebelling against its potential.

We must admit theatre's sphere is physical and plastic, not psychological. This does not simply mean assessing whether theatre's physical language can attain the same psychological resolutions as words or whether it can express emotions and feelings as well as words, but whether there are not attitudes in the field of intellect and thought which words cannot assume, which gestures and everything inclusive in this spatial language cannot attain with greater precision than them.

Before giving any examples of connections betwen the physical world and profound states of mind, I will quote what I wrote elsewhere:

"Any true feeling cannot in reality be expressed. To do so is to betray it. To express it, however, is to *conceal* it. True expression conceals what it exhibits. It pits the mind against nature's real vacuum, by creating in reaction a kind of fullness of thought. Or rather it creates a vacuum in thought, in relation to the manifest illusion of nature. Any strong feeling produces an idea of emptiness within us, and lucid language which prevents this emptiness also prevents poetry appearing in thought. For this reason an image, an allegory, a form disguising what it means to reveal, has more meaning to the mind than the enlightenment brought about by words or their analysis.

Hence true beauty never strikes us directly and the setting sun is beautiful because of everything else we lose by it."

The nightmares in Flemish painting are striking because they juxtapose the real world with a mere caricature of the world. They present us with spectres we encounter in our dreams. They originate in those same dream states which cause clumsy gestures and ridiculous slips of the tongue. They place a leaping harp beside a forgotten child; they show a real army advancing beneath the walls of a redoubtable fortress beside a human embryo carried along by underground rapids. Beside dreamt perplexity is the march of certainty, beyond yellow cavernous light the orange flash of a huge autumn sun about to set.

There is no question of abolishing speech in theatre but of changing its intended purpose, especially to lessen its status, to view it as something other than a way of guiding human nature to external ends, since our theatre is solely concerned with the way emotions and feelings conflict with one another or the way man is set against man in life.

Yet to change the purpose of theatre dialogue is to use it in an actual spatial sense, uniting it with everything in theatre that is spatial and significant in the tangible field. This means handling it as something concrete, disturbing things, first spatially, then in an infinitely more secret and mysterious field permitting more scope.

53

And it is not very hard to identify this extensive yet secretive field with that of formal anarchy on the one hand and also constant, formal creation on the other.

Thus, this identification of theatre's object with every possibility of formal, extensive manifestation, gives rise to the idea of a kind of spatial poetry, itself confused with enchantment.

In Oriental theatre with its metaphysical tendencies, as compared with Western theatre with its psychological tendencies, forms assume their meaning and significance on all possible levels. Or if you like, their pulsating results are not inferred merely on one level but on all mental levels at once.

And because of their manifold aspects, their disruptive strength and charm constantly stimulate the mind. Because Oriental theatre accepts the external appearance of things on several levels, because it does not restrict itself solely to the limitations or the impact of these aspects on the senses, but instead examines the degree of mental potential from which they have emerged, it shares in the intense poetry of nature and preserves its magical relationship with all the objective stages of universal mesmerism.

We ought to consider staging from the angle of magic and enchantment, not as reflecting a script, the mere projection of actual doubles arising from writing, but as the fiery projection of all the objective results of gestures, words, sounds, music or their combinations. This active projection can only occur on stage and its results can only be discovered from the auditorium or stage. And a playwright who uses nothing but words is not needed and must give way to specialists in objective, animated enchantment.

NO MORE MASTERPIECES

One of the reasons for the stifling atmosphere we live in, without any possible escape or remedy, which is shared by even the most revolutionary among us – is our respect for what has been written, expressed or painted, for whatever has taken shape, as if all expression were not finally exhausted, has not arrived at the point where things must break up to begin again, to make a fresh start.

We must finally do away with the idea of masterpieces reserved for a so-called elite but incomprehensible to the masses, since the mind has no red-light districts like those used for illicit sexual relations.

Past masterpieces are fit for the past, they are no good to us. We have the right to say what has been said and even what has not been said in a way that belongs to us, responding in a direct and straightforward manner to present-day feelings everybody can understand.

It is senseless to criticise the masses for having no sense of the sublime, when we ourselves confuse the sublime with one of those formal, moreover always dead exhibits. And if, for example, the masses today no longer understand *Oedipus Rex*, I would venture to say *Oedipus Rex* is at fault as a play and not the masses.

In *Oedipus Rex* there is the incest theme and the idea that nature does not give a rap for morality. And there are wayward

powers at large we would do well to be aware of, call them *fate* or what you will.

In addition, there is the presence of a plague epidemic which is the physical incarnation of these powers. But all this is clothed in language which has lost any contact with today's crude, epileptic rhythm. Sophocles may speak nobly, but in a manner that no longer suits the times. His speeches are too refined for today, as if he were speaking beside the point.

Yet the masses tremble at railway disasters, are familiar with earthquakes, plagues, revolutions and wars as well as being sensitive to the disturbing anguish of love and are capable of becoming conscious of all those grand ideas. They ask only to become conscious of them, but on condition we know how to speak their language and that notions of these things are not brought to them invested in a sophistication belonging to dead periods we will never relive.

Just as in former times, the masses today are thirsting for mystery. They only ask to become conscious of the laws by which fate reveals itself and perhaps to guess at the secret of its apparitions.

Let us leave textual criticism to teachers and formal criticism to aesthetes, and acknowledge that what has already been said no longer needs saying; that an expression twice used is of no value since it does not have two lives. Once spoken, all speech is dead and is only active as it is spoken. Once a form is used it has no more use, bidding man find another form, and theatre is the only place in the world where a gesture, once made, is never repeated in the same way.

If the masses do not frequent literary masterpieces, this is because the masterpieces are literary, that is to say set in forms no longer answering the needs of the times.

Far from accusing the masses, the public, we must accuse the formal screen we place between ourselves and the masses and that form of a new idolatry, the idolising of set masterpieces, an aspect

56

of middle-class conformity.

The conformity that makes us confuse the sublime, the concepts, and the objects with the forms they have acquired in our minds through the ages – our affected, snobbish, aesthetic mentality the public no longer understands.

It is useless in all this to accuse the public's bad taste while it slakes its thirst with inanities, as long as we have not given the public a worth-while show. And I defy anyone to point out a worth-while show *here*, worth-while in the highest sense of theatre, since the last great Romantic melodramas, that is a hundred years ago.

The public, which mistakes the bogus for truth, has the sense of what is true and always reacts to it when it appears. Today, however, we must look for it in the street, not on stage. And if the crowds in the street were given a chance to show their dignity as human beings, they would always do so.

If the masses have grown unused to going to the theatre, if we have all finally come to regard theatre as an inferior art, a means of coarse distraction, using it as an outlet for our worst instincts, this is because we have for too long been told theatre is all lies and illusion. Because for four hundred years, that is since the Renaissance, we have become accustomed to purely descriptive, narrative theatre, narrating psychology.

People exerted their ingenuity to bring to life on stage credible but detached beings, with the show on one side and the masses on the other – and the masses were shown only a mirror of themselves.

Shakespeare himself is responsible for this abberation and decline, this isolationist concept of theatre, holding that a stage performance ought not to affect the public, or that a projected image should not cause a shock to the anatomy, leaving an indelible impression on it.

If man in Shakespeare's plays is sometimes concerned with what is above him, it is always finally to determine the result of that concern within man, that is, psychology.

57

Psychology persists in bringing the unknown down to a level with the known, that is to say with the everyday and pedestrian. And psychology has caused this abasement and fearful loss of energy which appears to me to have really reached its limit. And it seems both theatre and ourselves want nothing more to do with psychology.

Besides, I think we are all agreed on this point of view and in order to censure psychological drama there is no need to stoop as low as disgusting modern French theatre.

Plots dealing with money, money troubles, social climbing, the pangs of love unspoilt by altruism, sexuality sugar-coated with eroticism yet shorn of mystery, are not theatre even if they are psychology. This anxiety, debauchery and lust, before which we are only Peeping Toms gratifying our instincts, tends to go sour and turn into revolution. This is something we must realise.

But that is not our most serious concern.

In the long run, Shakespeare and his followers have instilled a concept of art for art's sake in us, art on the one hand and life on the other, and we might rely on this lazy, ineffective idea as long as life outside held good, but there are too many signs that everything which used to sustain our lives no longer does so and we are all mad, desperate and sick. And I urge *us* to react.

This concept of unworldly art, charm-poetry existing solely to charm away the hours is a decadent notion, an unmistakable symptom of the emasculatory force within us.

Our literary admiration for Rimbaud, Jarry, Lautréamont and a few others, which drove two men to suicide, but turned into nothing more than café chit-chat for the rest, belongs to the idea of literary poetry, detached art, emasculated mental activity which has no effect and produces nothing. And I note that just when personal poetry, involving only its creator as he creates, became rife in a most excessive way, theatre was held in great contempt by poets who never had either a feeling for immediate group action, effectiveness or danger.

Let us do away with this foolish adherence to texts, to *written* poetry. Written poetry is valid once and then ought to be torn up. Let dead poets make way for the living. And we ought after all to be able to see it is our adulation for what has already been done, however fine and worthy it may be, that fossilises us, makes us stagnate and prevents us contacting that underlying power called thinking energy, vital power, determination of exchange, lunar periods or what have you. Poetry plain and simple, unformed and unwritten, underlies textual poetry. And just as masks, once used in magic rituals, are no longer fit for anything but to be put in museums – in the same way, the poetic effectiveness of a text is exhausted – theatre's effectiveness and poetry is exhausted least quickly of all, since it permits the action of movement and spoken things, never reproduced twice.

We must know what we want. If we are all prepared for war, the plague, famine and slaughter, we have no need to say so, we have only to go on as we are. To go on behaving as snobs, to flock to hear such and such a singer, to see such and such a wonderful show which never transcends the world of art (even the *Ballets Russes* at the height of their splendour never transcended the world of art), such and such an exhibition of painting where impressive forms dazzle us here and there, only by chance, and without being truly conscious of the powers they could arouse.

This empiricism, chance, personalism and anarchy must come to an end.

No more personal poems benefiting those who write them more than those who read them.

Once and for all, enough of these displays of closed, conceited, personal art.

Our anarchy and mental confusion are a function of the anarchy of everything else – or rather everything else is a function of that anarchy.

I am not of the opinion that civilisation must change so theatre can change, but I do believe theatre used in the highest and most

59

difficult sense has the power to affect the appearance and structure of things. And bringing two impassioned revelations together on stage, two living fires, two nervous magnetisms, is just as complete, as true, even as decisive as bringing together two bodies in short-lived debauchery is in life.

For this reason I suggest a Theatre of Cruelty.

With this mania we all have today for belittling everything, as soon as I said "cruelty" everyone took it to mean "blood". But a *"theatre of cruelty"* means theatre that is difficult and cruel for myself first of all. And on a performing level, it has nothing to do with the cruelty we practise on one another, hacking at each other's bodies, carving up our individual anatomies, or like, ancient Assyrian Emperors, posting sackfuls of human ears, noses or neatly dissected nostrils, but the far more terrible, essential cruelty objects can practise on us. We are not free and the sky can still fall on our heads. And above all else, theatre is made to teach us this.

Either we will be able to revert through theatre by present-day means to the higher idea of poetry underlying the Myths told by the great tragedians of ancient times, with theatre able once more to sustain a religious concept, that is to say without any meditation or useless contemplation, without diffuse dreams, to become conscious and also be in command of certain predominant powers, certain ideas governing everything; and since ideas, when they are effective generate their own energy, rediscover within us that energy which in the last analysis creates order and increases the value of life, or else we might as well abdicate now without protest, and acknowledge we are fit only for chaos, famine, bloodshed, war and epidemics.

Either we restore one focal attitude and necessity in all the arts, finding correspondences between a gesture in painting or on stage, and a gesture made by lava in a volcanic eruption, or we must stop painting, gossiping, writing or doing anything at all.

I suggest theatre today ought to return to the fundamental magic notion reintroduced by psychoanalysis, which consists in

60

curing a patient by making him assume the external attitude of the desired condition.

I suggest we ought to reject the empiricism of random images produced by the subconscious, calling them poetic and therefore hermetic images, as if that kind of trance brought about by poetry does not reverberate throughout our whole sensibility, in every nerve, as if poetry were a shadowy power with invariable motions.

I suggest we ought to return through theatre to the idea of a physical knowledge of images, a means of inducing trances, just as Chinese medicine knows the points of acupuncture over the whole extent of the human anatomy, down to our most sensitive functions.

Theatre can reinstruct those who have forgotten the communicative power or magic mimicry of gesture, because a gesture contains its own energy, and there are still human beings in theatre to reveal the power of these gestures.

To practice art is to deprive a gesture of its reverberations throughout the anatomy, whereas these reverberations, if the gesture is made in the conditions and with the force required, impels the anatomy and through it, the whole personality to adopt attitudes that correspond to that gesture.

Theatre is the only place in the world, the last group means we still possess of directly affecting the anatomy, and in neurotic, basely sensual periods like the one in which we are immersed, of attacking that base sensuality through physical means it cannot withstand.

Snakes do not react to music because of the mental ideas it produces in them, but because they are long, they lie coiled on the ground and their bodies are in contact with the ground along almost their entire length. And the musical vibrations communicated to the ground affect them as a very subtle, very long massage. Well I propose to treat the audience just like those charmed snakes and to bring them back to the subtlest ideas through their anatomies.

First of all by crude means, these gradually becoming more refined. But these crude, direct means hold its attention from the start.

61

For this reason the audience is in the centre in the "Theatre of Cruelty", while the show takes place around them.

In such a show there is continual amplification; the sounds, noises and cries are first sought for their vibratory qualities, secondly for what they represent.

Lighting occurs in its turn in these progressively refined means. Lighting made not only to give colour or to shed light, but containing its own force, influence and suggestiveness. For light in a green cave does not predispose the organism sensually in the same way as light on a very windy day.

Following on sound and lighting there is action and action's dynamism. This is where theatre, far from imitating life, communicates wherever it can with pure forces. And whether we accept or deny them, there is none the less a manner of speaking which gives the name forces to whatever gives birth to forceful images in our subconscious, to outwardly motiveless crime.

Violent, concentrated action is like lyricism; it calls forth supernatural imagery, a bloodshed of images, a bloody spirt of images inside the poet's head as well as in the audience's.

Whatever conflicts may obsess the mentality of the times, I defy any spectator infused with the blood of violent scenes, who has felt higher action pass through him, who has seen the rare, fundamental motions of his thought illuminated in extrordinary events – violence and bloodshed having been placed at the service of violence in thought – once outside the theatre, I defy him to indulge in thoughts of war, riot or motiveless murder.

The idea may seem puerile and advanced when stated in this way. And some will claim one example encourages another, that an attitude to cure encourages a cure, or murder to murder. Everything depends on the manner and purity with which things are done. There are risks. But we must not forget that while theatre action is violent it is not biased and theatre teaches us just how useless action is since once it is done it is over, as well as the superior use of that state of mind unused by action but which, if *turned about*, sublimates.

Therefore I propose a theatre where violent physical images pulverise, mesmerise the audience's sensibilities, caught in the drama as if in a vortex of higher forces.

Theatre, abandoning psychology, must narrate the unusual, stage nature's conflicts, nature's subtle powers arising first and foremost as extraordinary derivative powers. Theatre bringing on trances just as the whirling Dervishes or the Assouas induce trances. It must be aimed at the system by exact means, the same means as the sympathetic music used by some tribes which we admire on records but are incapable of originating among ourselves.

One runs risks, but I consider that in present-day conditions they are worth running. I do not believe we have succeeded in reanimating the world we live in and I also do not believe it worth hanging onto. But I propose something to get us out of the slump, instead of continuing to moan about it, about the boredom, dullness and stupidity of everything.

THEATRE AND CRUELTY

We have lost the idea of theatre. And in as much as theatre restricts itself to probing the intimacy of a few puppets, thereby transforming the audience into Peeping Toms, one understands why the elite have turned away from it or why the masses go to the cinema, music-hall and circus to find violent gratification whose intention does not disappoint them.

Our sensibility has reached the point where we surely need theatre that wakes us up heart and nerves.

The damage wrought by psychological theatre, derived from Racine, has rendered us unaccustomed to the direct, violent action theatre must have. Cinema in its turn, murders us with reflected, filtered and projected images that no longer *connect* with our sensibility, and for ten years has maintained us and all our faculties in an intellectual stupor.

In the anguished, catastrophic times we live in, we feel an urgent need for theatre that is not overshadowed by events, but arouses deep echoes within us and predominates over our unsettled period.

Our longstanding habit of seeking diversions has made us forget the slightest idea of serious theatre which upsets all our preconceptions, inspiring us with fiery, magnetic imagery and finally reacting on us after the manner of unforgettable soul therapy.

Everything that acts is cruelty. Theatre must rebuild itself on a concept of this drastic action pushed to the limit.

Infused with the idea that the masses think with their senses first and foremost and that it is ridiculous to appeal primarily to our understanding as we do in everyday psychological theatre, the Theatre of Cruelty proposes to resort to mass theatre, thereby rediscovering a little of the poetry in the ferment of great, agitated crowds hurled against one another, sensations only too rare nowadays, when masses of holiday crowds throng the streets.

If theatre wants to find itself needed once more, it must present everything in love, crime, war and madness.

Everyday love, personal ambition and daily worries are worthless except in relation to the kind of awful lyricism that exists in those Myths to which the great mass of men have consented.

This is why we will try to centre our show around famous personalities, horrible crimes and superhuman self-sacrifices, demonstrating that it can draw out the powers struggling within them, without resorting to the dead imagery of ancient Myths.

In a word, we believe there are living powers in what is called poetry, and that the picture of a crime presented in the right stage conditions is something infinitely more dangerous to the mind than if the same crime were committed in life.

We want to make theatre a believable reality inflicting this kind of tangible laceration, contained in all true feeling, on the heart and senses. In the same way as our dreams react on us and reality reacts on our dreams, so we believe ourselves able to associate mental pictures with dreams, effective in so far as they are projected with the required violence. And the audience will believe in the illusion of theatre on condition they really take it for a dream, nor for a servile imitation of reality. On condition it releases the magic freedom of daydreams, only recognisable when imprinted with terror and cruelty.

Hence this full scale invocation of cruelty and terror, its scope testing our entire vitality, confronting us with all our potential.

And in order to affect every facet of the spectator's sensibility, we advocate a revolving show, which instead of making stage and auditorium into two closed worlds without any possible communication between them, will extend its visual and oral outbursts over the whole mass of spectators.

Furthermore, leaving the field of analysible emotional feelings aside, we intend using the actor's lyricism to reveal external powers, and by this means to bring the whole of nature into the kind of theatre we would like to evoke.

However extensive a programme of this kind may be, it does not overreach theatre itself, which all in all seems to us to be associated with ancient magic powers.

Practically speaking, we want to bring back the idea of total theatre, where theatre will recapture from cinema, music-hall, the circus and life itself, those things that always belonged to it. This division between analytical theatre and a world of movement seems stupid to us. One cannot separate body and mind, nor the senses from the intellect, particularly in a field where the unendingly repeated jading of our organs calls for sudden shocks to revive our understanding.

Thus on the one hand we have the magnitude and scale of a show aimed at the whole anatomy, and on the other an intensive mustering of objects, gestures and signs used in a new spirit. The reduced role given to understanding leads to drastic curtailment of the script, while the active role given to dark poetic feeling necessitates tangible signs. Words mean little to the mind; expanded areas and objects speak out. New imagery speaks, even if composed in words. But spatial, thundering images replete with sound also speak, if we become versed in arranging a sufficient interjection of spatial areas furnished with silence and stillness.

We expect to stage a show based on these principles, where these direct active means are wholly used. Therefore such a show, unafraid of exploring the limits of our nervous sensibility, uses rhythm, sound, words, resounding with song, whose nature and startling combinations are part of an unrevealed technique.

Moreover, to speak clearly, the imagery in some paintings by Grunewald or Hieronymus Bosch gives us a good enough idea of what a show can be, where things in outside nature appear as temptations just as they would in a Saint's mind.

Theatre must rediscover its true meaning in this spectacle of a temptation, where life stands to lose everything and the mind to gain everything.

Besides we have put forward a programme which permits pure production methods discovered on the spot to be organised around historic or cosmic themes familiar to all.

And we insist that the first Theatre of Cruelty show will hinge on these mass concerns, more urgent and disturbing than any personal ones.

We must find out whether sufficient production means, financial or otherwise, can be found in Paris, before the cataclysm occurs, to allow such theatre (which must remain because it is the future) to come to life. Or whether real blood is needed right now to reveal this cruelty.

May 1933

THE THEATRE OF CRUELTY

First Manifesto

We cannot continue to prostitute the idea of theatre whose only value lies in its agonising magic relationship to reality and danger.

Put in this way, the problem of theatre must arouse universal attention, it being understood that theatre, through its physical aspect and because it requires *spatial expression* (the only real one in fact) allows the sum total of the magic means in the arts and words to be organically active like renewed exorcisms. From the foregoing it becomes apparent that theatre will never recover its own specific powers of action until it has also recovered its own language.

That is, instead of harking back to texts regarded as sacred and definitive, we must first break theatre's subjugation to the text and rediscover the idea of a kind of unique language somewhere in between gesture and thought.

We can only define this language as expressive, dynamic spatial potential in contrast with expressive spoken dialogue potential. Theatre can still derive possibilities for extension from speech outside words, the development in space of its dissociatory, vibratory action on our sensibility. We must take inflexion into account here, the particular way a word is pronounced, as well as the visual

68

language of things (audible, sound language aside), also movement, attitudes and gestures, providing their meanings are extended, their features connected even as far as those signs, making a kind or alphabet out of those signs. Having become conscious of this spatial language, theatre owes it to itself to organise these shouts, sounds, lights and onomatopoeic language, creating true hieroglyphs out of characters and objects, making use of their symbolism and interconnections in relation to every organ and on all levels.

Therefore we must create word, gesture and expressive metaphysics, in order to rescue theatre from its human, psychological prostration. But all this is of no use unless a kind of real metaphysical temptation, invoking certain unusual notions, lies behind such an effort, for the latter by their very nature cannot be restricted or even formally depicted. These ideas on Creation, Growth and Chaos are all of a cosmic order, giving us an initial idea of a field now completely alien to theatre. They can create a kind of thrilling equation between Man, Society, Nature and Objects.

Anyhow, there is no question of putting metaphysical ideas directly on stage but of creating kinds of temptations, vacuums, around these ideas. Humour and its anarchy, poetry and its symbolism and imagery, give us a kind of primary idea of how to channel the temptation in these ideas.

Here we ought to mention the purely physical side of this language, that is to say all the ways and means it has of acting on our sensibility.

It would be futile to say it calls on music, dancing, mime or mimicry. Obviously it uses moves, harmonies, rhythms, but only up to the point where they can co-operate in a kind of pivotal expression without favouring any particular art. However this does not mean it omits ordinary facts and emotions, but it uses them as a springboard in the same way as HUMOUR as DESTRUCTION can serve to reconcile laughter with our reasoning habits.

But this tangible, objective theatre language captivates and bewitches our senses by using a truly Oriental concept of expression.

69

It runs through our sensibility. Abandoning our Western ideas of speech, it turns words into incantation. It expands the voice. It uses vocal vibrations and qualities, wildly trampling them underfoot. It pile-drives sounds. It aims to exalt, to benumb, to bewitch, to arrest our sensibility. It liberates a new lyricism of gestures which because it is distilled and spatially amplified, ends by surpassing the lyricism of words. Finally it breaks away from language's intellectual subjugation by conveying the sense of a new, deeper intellectualism hidden under these gestures and signs and raised to the dignity of special exorcisms.

For all this magnetism, all this poetry, all these immediately bewitching means would be to no avail if they did not put the mind bodily on the track of something, if true theatre could not give us the sense of a creation where we are in possession of only one of its facets, while its completion exists on other levels.

And it makes no difference whether these other levels are really conquered by the mind, that is to say by our intellect, for this curtails them, a pointless and meaningless act. What matters is that our sensibility is put into a deeper, subtler state of perception by assured means, the very object of magic and ritual, of which theatre is only a reflection.

TECHNIQUE

The problem is to turn theatre into a function in the proper sense of the word, something as exactly localised as the circulation of our blood through our veins, or the apparently chaotic evolution of dream images in the mind, by an effective mix, truly enslaving our attention.

Theatre will never be itself again, that is to say will never be able to form truly illusive means, unless it provides the audience with truthful distillations of dreams where its taste for crime, its erotic obsessions, its savageness, its fantasies, its utopian sense of

70

life and objects, even its cannibalism, do not gush out on an illusory, make-believe, but on an inner level.

In other words, theatre ought to pursue a re-examination not only of all aspects of an objective, descriptive outside world, but also all aspects of an inner world, that is to say man viewed metaphysically, by every means at its disposal. We believe that only in this way will we be able to talk about imagination's rights in the theatre once more. Neither Humour, Poetry or Imagination mean anything unless they re-examine man organically through anarchic destruction, his ideas on reality and his poetic position in reality, generating stupendous flights of forms constituting the whole show.

But to view theatre as a second-hand psychological or moral operation and to believe dreams themselves only serve as a substitute is to restrict both dreams' and theatre's deep poetic range. If theatre is as bloody and as inhuman as dreams, the reason for this is that it perpetuates the metaphysical notions in some Fables in a present-day, tangible manner, whose atrocity and energy are enough to prove their origins and intentions in fundamental first principles rather than to reveal and unforgettably tie down the idea of continual conflict within us, where life is continually lacerated, where everything in creation rises up and attacks our condition as created beings.

This being so, we can see that by its proximity to the first principles poetically infusing it with energy, this naked theatre language, a non-virtual but real language using man's nervous magnetism, must allow us to transgress the ordinary limits of art and words, actively, that is to say magically to produce a kind of total creation *in real terms*, where man must reassume his position between dreams and events.

SUBJECTS

We do not mean to bore the audience to death with transcendental

71

cosmic preoccupations. Audiences are not interested whether there are profound clues to the show's thought and action, since in general this does not concern them. But these must still be there and that concerns us.

*

The Show: Every show will contain physical, objective elements perceptible to all. Shouts, groans, apparitions, surprise, dramatic moments of all kinds, the magic beauty of the costumes modelled on certain ritualistic patterns, brilliant lighting, vocal, incantational beauty, attractive harmonies, rare musical notes, object colours, the physical rhythm of the moves whose build and fall will be wedded to the beat of moves familiar to all, the tangible appearance of new, surprising objects, masks, puppets many feet high, abrupt lighting changes, the physical action of lighting stimulating heat and cold, and so on.

Staging: This archetypal theatre language will be formed around staging not simply viewed as one degree of refraction of the script on stage, but as the starting point for theatrical creation. And the old duality between author and producer will disappear, to be replaced by a kind of single Creator using and handling this language, responsible both for the play and the action.

Stage Language: We do not intend to do away with dialogue, but to give words something of the significance they have in dreams.

Moreover we must find new ways of recording this language, whether these ways are similar to musical notation or to some kind of code.

As to ordinary objects, or even the human body, raised to the dignity of signs, we can obviously take our inspiration from hieroglyphic characters not only to transcribe these signs legibly so they can be reproduced at will, but to compose exact symbols on stage that are immediately legible.

72

lary that all objects requiring a stereotyped physical repr   s
will be discarded or disguised.

Decor: No decor. Hieroglyphic characters, ritual costume, t
foot high effigies of King Lear's beard in the storm, musical inst
ments as tall as men, objects of unknown form and purpose ar
enough to fulfill this function.

Topicality: But, you may say, theatre so removed from life, facts
or present-day activities . . . news and events, yes! Anxieties, whatever is profound about them, the prerogative of the few, no! In the
Zohar, the story of the Rabbi Simeon is as inflammatory as fire,
as topical as fire.

Works: We will not act written plays but will attempt to stage
productions straight from subjects, facts or known works. The type
and lay-out of the auditorium itself governs the show as no theme,
however vast, is precluded to us.

Show: We must revive the concept of an integral show. The problem is to express it, spatially nourish and furnish it like tap-holes
drilled into a flat wall of rock, suddenly generating geysers and
bouquets of stone.

The Actor: The actor is both a prime factor, since the show's
success depends on the effectiveness of his acting, as well as a kind
of neutral, pliant factor since he is rigorously denied any individual
initiative. Besides, this is a field where there are no exact rules. And
there is a wide margin dividing a man from an instrument, between
an actor required to give nothing more than a certain number of
sobs and one who has to deliver a speech, using his own powers of
persuasion.

Interpretation: The show will be coded from start to finish, like a

Then again, this coding and musical notation will be valuable as
a means of vocal transcription.

Since the basis of this language is to initiate a special use of
inflexions, these must take up a kind of balanced harmony, a sub-
sidary exaggeration of speech able to be reproduced at will.

Similarly the thousand and one facial expressions caught in the
form of masks, can be listed and labelled so they may directly and
symbolically participate in this tangible stage language, independently of their particular psychological use.

Furthermore, these symbolic gestures, masks, postures, individual or group moves, whose countless meanings constitute an
important part of the tangible stage language of evocative gestures,
emotive arbitrary postures, the wild pounding of rhythms and
sound, will be multiplied, added to by a kind of mirroring of the
gestures and postures, consisting of the accumulation of all the
impulsive gestures, all the abortive postures, all the lapses in the
mind and of the tongue by which speech's incapabilities are revealed, and on occasion we will not fail to turn to this stupendous
existing wealth of expression.

Besides, there is a tangible idea of music where sound enters
like a character, where harmonies are cut in two and become lost
precisely as words break in.

Connections, levels, are established between one means of
expression and another; even lighting can have a predetermined
intellectual meaning.

Musical Instruments: These will be used as objects, as part of the
set.

Moreover they need to act deeply and directly on our sensibility
through the senses, and from the point of view of sound they invite
research into utterly unusual sound properties and vibrations which
present-day musical instruments do not possess, urging us to use
ancient or forgotten instruments or to invent new ones. Apart from
music, research is also needed into instruments and appliances

based on special refining and new alloys which can reach a new scale in the octave and produce an unbearably piercing sound or noise.

Lights – Lighting: The lighting equipment currently in use in the theatre is no longer adequate. The particular action of light on the mind comes into play, we must discover oscillating light effects, new ways of diffusing lighting in waves, sheet lighting like a flight of fire-arrows. The colour scale of the equipment currently in use must be revised from start to finish. Fineness, density and opacity factors must be reintroduced into lighting, so as to produce special tonal properties, sensations of heat, cold, anger, fear and so on.

Costume: As to costume, without believing there can be any uniform stage costume that would be the same for all plays, modern dress will be avoided as much as possible not because of a fetishistic superstition for the past, but because it is perfectly obvious certain age-old costumes of ritual intent, although they were once fashionable, retain a revealing beauty and appearance because of their closeness to the traditions which gave rise to them.

The Stage – The Auditorium: We intend to do away with stage and auditorium, replacing them by a kind of single, undivided locale without any partitions of any kind and this will become the very scene of the action. Direct contact will be established between the audience and the show, between actors and audience, from the very fact that the audience is seated in the centre of the action, is encircled and furrowed by it. This encirclement comes from the shape of the house itself.

Abandoning the architecture of present-day theatres, we will rent some kind of barn or hangar rebuilt along lines culminating in the architecture of some churches, holy places, or certain Tibetan temples.

This building will have special interior height and depth dimen-

74

ions. The auditorium will be enclosed within four walls stripped of any ornament, with the audience seated below, in the middle, on swivelling chairs allowing them to follow the show taking place around them. In effect, the lack of a stage in the normal sense of the word will permit the action to extend itself to the four corners of the auditorium. Special places will be set aside for the actors and action in the four cardinal points of the hall. Scenes will be acted in front of washed walls designed to absorb light. In addition, overhead galleries run right around the circumference of the room as in some Primitive paintings. These galleries will enable actors to pursue one another from one corner of the hall to the other as needed, and the action can extend in all directions at all perspective levels of height and depth. A shout could be transmitted by word of mouth from one end to the other with a succession of amplifications and inflexions. The action will unfold, extending its trajectory from floor to floor, from place to place, with sudden outbursts flaring up in different spots like conflagrations. And the show's truly illusive nature will not be empty words any more than the action's direct, immediate hold on the spectators. For the action, diffused over a vast area, will require the lighting for one scene and the varied lighting for a performance to hold the audience as well as the characters – and physical lighting methods, the thunder and wind whose repercussions will be experienced by the spectators, will correspond with several actions at once, several phases in one action with the characters clinging together like swarms, will endure all the onslaughts of the situations and the external assaults of weather and storms.

However, a central site will be retained which, without acting as a stage properly speaking, enables the body of the action to be concentrated and brought to a climax whenever necessary.

Objects – Masks – Props: Puppets, huge masks, objects of strange proportions appear by the same right as verbal imagery, stressing the physical aspect of all imagery and expression – with the corol-

75

language. Thus no moves will be wasted, all obeying a rhythm, every character being typified to the limit, each gesture, feature and costume to appear as so many shafts of light.

Cinema: Through poetry, theatre contrasts pictures of the unformulated with the crude visualisation of what exists. Besides, from an action viewpoint, one cannot compare a cinema image, however poetic it may be, since it is restricted by the film, with a theatre image which obeys all life's requirements.

Cruelty: There can be no spectacle without an element of cruelty as the basis of every show. In our present degenerative state, metaphysics must be made to enter the mind through the body.

The Audience: First, this theatre must exist.

Programme: Disregarding the text, we intend to stage:
1. An adaptation of a Shakespearean work, absolutely consistent with our present confused state of mind, whether this be an apocryphal Shakespeare play such as *Arden of Faversham* or another play from that period.
2. A very free poetic play by Léon-Paul Fargue.
3. An excerpt from *The Zohar*, the Story of Rabbi Simeon which has the ever-present force and virulence of a conflagration.
4. The story of Bluebeard, reconstructed from historical records, containing a new concept of cruelty and eroticism.
5. The Fall of Jerusalem, according to the Bible and the Scriptures. On the one hand a blood red colour flowing from it, that feeling of running wild and mental panic visible even in daylight. On the other hand, the prophets' metaphysical quarrels, with the dreadful intellectual agitation they cause, their reaction rebounding bodily on the King, the Temple, the Masses and Events.
6. One of the Marquis de Sade's tales, its eroticism transposed, allegorically represented and cloaked in the sense of a violent

externalisation of cruelty, masking the remainder.

7. One or more Romantic melodramas where the unbelievable will be an active, tangible, poetic factor.

8. Buchner's *Woyzeck* in a spirit of reaction against our principles, and as an example of what can be drawn from an exact text in terms of the stage.

9. Elizabethan theatre works stripped of the lines, retaining only their period machinery, situations, character and plot.

LETTERS OF CRUELTY

First Letter

Paris, September 13, 1932

To J.P.

My Dear Friend,

I can give you no details about my Manifesto without spoiling its emphasis. All I can do for the time being is to make a few remarks to try and justify my choice of title, the Theatre of Cruelty.

This cruelty is not sadistic or bloody, at least not exclusively so.

I do not systematically cultivate horror. The word cruelty must be taken in its broadest sense, not in the physical, predatory sense usually ascribed to it. And in so doing, I demand the right to make a break with its usual verbal meaning, to break the bonds once and for all, to break asunder the yoke, finally to return to the etymological origins of language, which always evoke a tangible idea through abstract concepts.

One may perfectly well envisage pure cruelty without any carnal laceration. Indeed, philosophically speaking, what is cruelty? From a mental viewpoint, cruelty means strictness, diligence, unrelenting decisiveness, irreversible and absolute determination.

From the aspect of our own existence, the most current philosophical determinism is an image of cruelty.

We are wrong to make cruelty mean merciless bloodshed, pointless pursuits unrelated to physical ills. The Ethiopian Ra, carting off defeated princes and imposing servitude on them was not driven to do so by a desperate thirst for blood. In fact, cruelty is

79

not synonymous with bloodshed, martyred flesh or crucified enemies. Associating cruelty and torture is only one minor aspect of the problem. Practising cruelty involves a higher determination to which the executioner-tormentor is also subject and which he must be *resolved* to endure when the time comes. Above all, cruelty is very lucid, a kind of strict control and submission to necessity. There is no cruelty without consciousness, without the application of consciousness, for the latter gives practising any act in life a blood red tinge, its cruel overtones, since it is understood that being alive always means the death of someone else.

Second Letter

Paris, November 14, 1932

To J.P.

My Dear Friend,

Cruelty is not an adjunct to my thoughts, it has always been there, but I had to become conscious of it. I use the word cruelty in the sense of hungering after life, cosmic strictness, relentless necessity, in the Gnostic sense of a living vortex engulfing darkness, in the sense of the inescapably necessary pain without which life could not continue. Good has to be desired, it is the result of an act of willpower, while evil is continuous. When the hidden god creates, he obeys a cruel need for creation imposed on him, yet he cannot avoid creating, thus permitting an ever more condensed, ever more consumed nucleus of evil to enter the eye of the willed vortex of good. Theatre in the sense of constant creation, a wholly magic act, obeys this necessity. A play without this desire, this blind zest for life, capable of surpassing everything seen in every gesture or every act, in the transcendant aspect of the plot, would be useless and a failure as theatre.

THE THEATRE OF CRUELTY

Second Manifesto

Whether they admit it or not, whether a conscious or unconscious act, at heart audiences are searching for a poetic state of mind, a transcendant condition by means of love, crime, drugs, war or insurrection.

The Theatre of Cruelty was created in order to restore an impassioned convulsive concept of life to theatre, and we ought to accept the cruelty on which this is based in the sense of drastic strictness, the extreme concentration of stage elements.

This cruelty will be bloody if need be, but not systematically so, and will therefore merge with the idea of a kind of severe mental purity, not afraid to pay the cost one must pay in life.

1. Inner Meaning

That is to say the subjects and themes dealt with.

The Theatre of Cruelty will choose themes and subjects corresponding to the agitation and unrest of our times.

It does not intend to leave the task of revealing man or life's contemporary Myths to the cinema. But it will do so in its own way, that is to say, contrary to the world slipping into an economic, utilitarian and technological state, it will bring major considerations

81

and fundamental emotions back into style, since modern theatre has overlaid these with the veneer of pseudo-civilised man.

These themes will be universal, cosmic, performed according to the most ancient texts taken from Mexican, Hindu, Judaic and Iranian cosmogonies, among others.

Repudiating psychological man with his clear-cut personality and feelings, it will appeal to the whole man, not social man submissive to the law, warped by religions and precepts.

And both the upper and lower strata of the mind will play their part. The reality of the imagination and dreams will appear on a par with life.

In addition, great social upheavals, clashes between peoples, natural forces, the interventions of chance, the attractions of fate will all appear either directly in the movements and gestures of the characters elevated in stature like gods, heroes or monsters of legendary size, or else directly in material form obtained by new scientific processes.

These gods or heroes, these monsters, these natural, cosmic forces will be depicted according to pictures in the most venerable holy books or ancient cosmogonies.

2. Form

Furthermore, theatre's need to steep itself in the wellsprings of infinitely stirring and sensitive poetry, to reach the furthest removed, the most backward and inattentive part of the audience, achieved by a return to ancient primal Myths, not through the script but the production, will not be solely required to incarnate and particularly to bring these ancient conflicts *up to date*. That is to say, the themes will be transferred straight on stage but incarnated in moves, expressions and gestures, before gushing out in words.

In this way we can repudiate theatre's superstition concerning the script and the author's autocracy.

In this way also we will link up with popular, primal theatre sensed and experienced directly by the mind, without language's distortions and the pitfalls in speech and words.

Above all, we intend to base theatre on the show and we will bring a new concept of space into the show; all possible levels, all possible height and depth sight-lines must be used, and a special notion of time coupled with movement will exist within this concept.

In addition to the greatest possible number of moves in a given time, the greatest possible amount of physical imagery and meaning must be combined with these moves.

The moves and imagery used will not exist solely to please eye and ear, but more profitably to please the intimate self, the mind.

Thus stage space will not only be measured by size or volume but from what one might term *a mysterious aspect*.

The overlapping of imagery and moves must culminate in a genuine physical language, no longer based on words but on signs formed through the combination of objects, silence, shouts and rhythms.

For it must be understood, we intend to introduce silence and rhythm into the great number of moves and images arranged within a given time as well as a certain physical pulsation and excitement, composed of really created, really used objects and gestures. One could say the spirit of the most ancient hieroglyphics will govern the creation of this pure stage language.

All popular audiences have always been fond of direct expression and imagery; spoken words and explicit verbal expression occur in all the clearest and most distinctly elucidated parts of the plot, those parts where life is lulled to sleep and consciousness takes over.

And words will be construed in an incantatory, truly magical sense, side by side with this logical sense – not only for their meaning, but for their forms, their sensual radiation.

83

For the actual appearance of these monsters, orgies of heroes and gods, a plastic revelation of powers, explosive interjections of poetry and humour, whose task is to disorganise and pulverise appearances in accordance with the analagous, anarchic principle of all true poetry, will only possess true magic in a hypnotically suggestive mood where the mind is affected by direct sensual pressure.

If the nerves, that is to say a certain physiological sensitivity are deliberately omitted from today's after-dinner theatre, or left to the spectator's personal interpretation, the Theatre of Cruelty intends to return to all the tried and tested magic means of affecting sensitivity.

These means, consisting of differing intensities of colour, light or sound, using vibrations and tremors, musical, rhythmic repetition or the repetition of spoken phrases, bringing tonality or a general diffusion of light into play, can only achieve their full effect by using *discords*.

But instead of restricting these discords to dominating one sense alone, we mean to make them overlap from one sense to another, from colour to sound, words to lighting, tremoring gestures to tonality soaring with sound, and so on.

By eliminating the stage, shows made up and constructed in this manner will extend over the whole auditorium and will scale the walls from the ground up along slender catwalks, physically enveloping the audience, constantly immersing them in light, imagery movements and sound. The set will consist of the characters themselves, grown as tall as gigantic puppets, landscapes of moving lights playing on objects, or continually shifting masks.

And just as there are to be no empty spatial areas, there must be no let up, no vacuum in the audience's mind or sensitivity. That is to say there will be no distinct divisions, no gap between life and theatre. Anyone who has watched a scene of any film being shot, will understand just what I mean.

We want to have the same material means, lighting, extras and resources at our disposal for a stage show, as are daily squandered on reels of film, where everything that is active and magic about such a display is lost for ever.

*

The first Theatre of Cruelty show will be entitled:

THE CONQUEST OF MEXICO

This will stage events rather than men. Men will appear in their proper place with their emotions and psychology interpreted as the emergence of certain powers in the light of the events and historical destiny in which they played their role.

The subject was chosen:

1. Because it involves the present, and because of all the references it allows to problems of vital interest both to Europe and the world.

From a historical point of view, *The Conquest of Mexico* raises the question of colonisation. It revives Europe's deep-rooted self-conceit in a burning, inexorably bloody manner, allowing us to debunk its own concept of its supremacy. It contrasts Christianity with far older religions. It treats the false conceptions the West has somehow formed concerning paganism and other natural religions with the contempt they deserve, emphasising with burning emotion, the splendour and ever present poetry of the ancient metaphysical foundations on which these religions were built.

2. By raising the dreadfully contemporary problem of colonisation, that is the right one continent considers it has to enslave another, it questions the real supremacy some races may have over others, showing the inner filiation linking a race's genius with particular forms of civilisation. It contrasts the tyrannical anarchy of the colonisors with the deep intellectual concord of those about to be colonised.

Further, by comparison with the European monarchical chaos at

85

that time, based on the most unjust and dull-witted materialistic principles, it sheds light on the organic hierarchy of the Aztec monarchy established on indisputable spiritual principles.

From a social point of view, it demonstrates the peacefulness of a society which knew how to feed all its members and where the Revolution had taken place at its inception.

From the clash between the mental chaos in Catholic anarchy and pagan order, this subject can set off unbelievable holocausts of power and imagery, interspersed here and there with abrupt dialogue, hand to hand combat between men bearing the most opposed ideas within them like stigmata.

The inner mental meaning and the current interest in such a show having been sufficiently emphasised, we intend to highlight the *spectacular* merit of the conflicts it will stage.

First there is Montezuma's inner struggle, a king torn in two, history having been unable to enlighten us on his motives.

We will show his inner struggle, and his symbolic discussion with visualised astronomical myths in a pictorial, objective manner.

Finally, aside from Montezuma, there are the masses, the different social strata; the masses rising up against fate represented by Montezuma, the clamouring of the sceptics, quibbling philosophers and priests, the lamentations of the poets, middle-class and merchant treachery, the duplicity and sexual listlessness of the women.

The mentality of the masses, the spirit of events, will travel over the show in material waves, determining certain lines of force, and the diminished, rebelled or despairing consciousness of individuals will be carried along like straws.

Theatrically, the problem is to determine and harmonise these lines of force, to focus them and to obtain suggestive melodies from them.

These images, moves, dances, rituals, music, melodies cut short, and sudden turns of dialogue will all be carefully recorded and described as far as one can in words, especially in the non-speaking parts of the show, the rule being to succeed in recording or codifying anything that cannot be described in words, just like in a musical score.

AN AFFECTIVE ATHLETICISM

One must grant the actor a kind of affective musculature matching the bodily localisation of our feelings.

An actor is like a physical athlete, with this astonishing corollary; his affective organism is similar to the athlete's, being parallel to it like a double, although they do not act on the same level.

The actor is a heart athlete.

In his case the whole man is also separated into three worlds; the affective area is his own.

It belongs to him organically.

The muscular movements of physical exertion are a likeness, a double of another exertion, located in the same points as stage acting movements.

The actor relies on the same pressure points an athlete relies on to run, in order to hurl a convulsive curse whose course is driven inward.

Similar anatomical bases can be found in all the feints in boxing, all-in-wrestling, the hundred metres, the high jump and the movements of the emotions, since they all have the same physical support points.

With this further rider that the moves are reversed and in anything to do with breathing, for instance, an actor's body relies on breathing while with a wrestler, a physical athlete, the breathing relies on his body.

The question of breathing is of prime importance; it is inversely proportional to external expression.

The more inward and restrained the expression, the more ample, concentrated and substantial breathing becomes, full of resonances.

Whereas breathing is compressed in short waves for ample, fiery externalised acting.

We can be sure that every mental movement, every feeling, every leap in human affectivity has an appropriate breath.

These breathing *tempi* have a name taught us by the Cabala, for they form the human heart and the gender of our emotional activity.

An actor is merely a crude empiricist, a practitioner guided by vague instinct.

Yet on no consideration does this mean we should teach him to rave.

What is at stake is to end this kind of wild ignorance in the midst of which all present theatre moves, as if through a haze, constantly faltering. A gifted actor instinctively knows how to tap and radiate certain powers. But he would be astonished if he were told those powers which make their own substantial journey *through the senses* existed, for he never realised they could actually exist.

To use his emotions in the same way as a boxer uses his muscles, he must consider a human being as a Double, like the Kha of the Egyptian mummies, like an eternal ghost radiating affective powers.

As a supple, never-ending apparition, a form aped by the true actor, imposing the forms and picture of his own sensibility on it.

Theatre has an effect on this Double, this ghostly effigy it moulds, and like all ghosts this apparition has a long memory. The heart's memory endures and an actor certainly thinks with his heart, for his heart holds sway.

This means that in theatre more than anywhere else, an actor must become conscious of the emotional world, not by attributing imaginary merits to it, but those with concrete meaning.

Whether this hypothesis is exact or not, the main thing is that it can be authenticated.

The soul can be physiologically summarised as a maze of vibrations.

This ghostly soul can be regarded as exhilarated by its own cries, otherwise what are the Hindu mantras, those consonances, those strange stresses where the soul's secret side is hounded down into its innermost lairs, to reveal its secrets publicly.

Belief in the soul's flowing substantiality is essential to the actor's craft. To know that an emotion is substantial, subject to the plastic vicissitudes of matter, gives him control over his passions, extending our sovereign command.

To arrive at the emotions through their powers instead of regarding them as pure extraction, confers a mastery on an actor equal to a true healer's.

To know there is a physical outlet for the soul permits him to journey down into that soul in a reverse direction as well as to discover existence by calculated analogies.

To understand the mystery of passionate *time*, a kind of musical *tempo* conducting its harmonic beat, is an aspect of the drama modern psychological theatre has certainly disregarded for some time.

Now this *tempo* can be rediscovered analogically; it is to be found in the six ways of distributing and conserving breath as if it were a precious element.

All breathing has three measures, just as there are three basic principles in all creation, and the figures that correspond to them can be found in breathing itself.

The Cabala divides human breathing into six main arcana, the first, called the Great Arcanum, is creation:

ANDROGYNOUS	MALE	FEMALE
BALANCED	EXPANDING	ATTRACTING
NEUTER	POSITIVE	NEGATIVE

Therefore I thought of using a science of types of breathing, not only for an actor's work, but also in preparing him for his craft. For if a science of breathing sheds light on the tenor of the soul, it can stimulate the soul all the more by aiding it to flourish.

We can be sure that since breathing accompanies exertion, automatically produced breathing will give rise to a corresponding quality of exertion in the straining anatomy.

The exertion will have the tenor and rhythm of this artificially produced breathing.

Exertion sympathetically accompanies breathing, and according to the quality of the exertion to be produced, a preparatory projection of breathing will make this exertion easy and spontaneous. I stress the word spontaneous, since breathing revives life, infusing fire into its matter.

This voluntary breathing incites the spontaneous reappearance of life. Like a many-coloured voice, warriors are sleeping at its edges. Matins or trumpet calls make them hurl themselves in ranks into the fray. But if a child suddenly cries "wolf" those same warriors awaken. Waken in the dead of night. False alarm; the soldiers are returning. No, they run into enemy units, falling into a real hornet's nest. The child cried out in his dreams. His supersensitive, hovering subconscious had run into a band of enemies. Thus in round-about ways, fiction provoked by the drama lights on a reality deadlier than the former and unsuspected by life.

Thus an actor delves down into his personality by the whetted edge of his breathing.

For breathing which maintains life, allows us to climb its stages step by step. If an actor does not have a certain feeling, he can probe it again through breathing, on the condition he judiciously combines its effects, without mistaking its gender. For breathing is either male or female, less often bi-sexual. One may even have to portray some rare, fixed condition.

Breathing accompanies feeling and the actor can penetrate this feeling through breathing, provided he knows how to distinguish which breathing suits which feeling.

As indicated above, there are six main breathing combinations:

NEUTER	MASCULINE	FEMININE
NEUTER	FEMININE	MASCULINE
MASCULINE	NEUTER	FEMININE
FEMININE	NEUTER	MASCULINE
MASCULINE	FEMININE	NEUTER
FEMININE	MASCULINE	NEUTER

And a seventh state higher than breathing, uniting the revealed and the unrevealed through the portals of a higher Guna, the state of Sattva.

Should someone maintain an actor is not essentially a metaphysician and that this seventh state does not concern him, our answer is that if theatre is the most perfect and complete symbol of universal revelation, an actor bears the principle of this seventh state within him, this bloody artery along which he probes all the others, everytime his controlled organs wake from their slumbers.

Surely instinct is there most of the time to make up for this absence of an undefinable idea. No need to fall as low as the ordinary emotions which fill current theatre. Moreover this breathing method was not devised for ordinary emotions. And rehearsed, cultivated breathing, following a method often used, was not made merely to prepare us for a declaration of adulterous love.

When an exhalation is rehearsed seven or twelve times it prepares us for the subtle quality of an outcry, for desperate soul demands.

We localise this breathing, distributing it between contracted and decontracted states. We use our bodies like screens through which will-power and relinquished will-power pass.

The tempo of voluntary thought makes us powerfully project a male beat, followed by a prolonged feminine beat without too apparent a transition.

The tempo of involuntary thought or even no thought at all and exhausted feminine breathing makes us inhale suffocating cellar heat, a monsoon wind, and on the same prolonged beat we exhale heavily. Yet throughout our whole body quivering by areas, our muscles never stopped functioning.

The main thing it to become conscious of these localisations of affective thought. One way of recognising them is by exertion. The same pressure points which support physical exertion are also used in the emergence of affective thought. The same also act as a jumping-off point for the emergence of a feeling.

We ought to note that everything feminine, everything which is surrender, anguish, a plea, an invocation, stretching out towards something in a gesture of supplication, also rests on exertion pressure points, only like a diver who touches the sea bed to rise to the surface. A kind of vacuum ray remains where the tension had been.

But in this case the masculine returns to haunt the feminine's place like a shadow. Whereas, when the affective condition is male, the interior body consists of a kind of inverted geometry, a picture of the condition reversed.

To become conscious of physical obsession, muscles brushed by emotion, amounts to unleashing that emotion powerfully, and just as in active breathing, gives it secret, deep, unusually violent volume.

From the above it seems clear that any actor, even the least gifted, can increase the inner density and amplitude of his feelings through this physical science, and that a fuller expression follows this organic assumption.

It would do no harm for our purposes to become familiar with a few localised points.

Weight-lifters lift with their backs, arching their backs to support the additional strength in their arms. And curiously enough one inversely ascertains that every feminine draining feeling; sobs, sorrow, fitful pouting, fright, all this vacuum occurs in the small of the back, the very spot where Chinese acupuncture relieves congested kidneys. For Chinese medicine operates only according to fullness and emptiness. Convex and concave. Tense or relaxed. *Yin and Yang*. Masculine and Feminine.

There is another radiating pressure point; anger, bite and attack are located in the centre of the solar plexus. The brain relies on this point to eject its mental venom.

The point of heroism and the sublime is also that of guilt, where we strike our breasts, where anger boils up, raging but never advancing.

For wherever anger advances, guilt recedes; this is the secret of fullness and emptiness.

Acute, self-mutilating anger begins with a cracking neuter, becomes localised in the solar plexus by a swift feminine void, is clamped on both shoulderblades, then comes back like a boomerang, erupting sparks which burn themselves out without continuing. Although they lose their corrosive emphasis they retain the correlation of male breathing and die out furiously.

I wanted to restrict myself to examples bearing on the few fertile principles comprising the material of this technical essay. Others, if they have time, can draw up the complete structure of the method. There are 380 points in Chinese acupuncture, with 73 major ones in normal therapy, but there are far fewer crude outlets for human emotions.

We can indicate far fewer pressure points on which to base the soul's athleticism.

The secret is to irritate those pressure points as if the muscles

94

were flayed.

The rest is achieved by screams.

*

To reforge the links, the chain of a rhythm when audiences saw their own real lives in a show. We must allow audiences to identify with the show breath by breath and beat by beat.

It is not enough for the audience to be riveted by the show's magic and this will never happen unless we know where *to affect them*. We have had enough of chance magic or poetry which has no skill underlying it.

In theatre, poetry and skill must be associated as one from now on.

Every emotion has an organic basis and an actor charges his emotional voltage by developing his emotions within him.

The key to throwing the audience into a magical trance is to know in advance what pressure points must be affected in the body. But theatre poetry has long become unaccustomed to this invaluable kind of skill.

To be familiar with the points of localisation in the body is to reforge the magic links.

Using breathing's hieroglyphics, I can rediscover a concept of divine theatre.

N.B. – In Europe no one knows how to scream any more, particularly actors in a trance no longer know how to cry out, since they do nothing but talk, having forgotten they have a body on stage, they have also lost the use of their throats. Abnormally shrunk, these throats are no longer organs but monstrous, talking abstractions. French actors now only know how to talk.

SERAPHIM'S THEATRE

To Jean Paulhan

There are enough details for one to understand.
To be more explicit would spoil *its poetry.*

NEUTER
FEMININE
MASCULINE

I want to attempt a terrific feminine. The cry of claims, of trampled down rebellion, of steeled anguish at war.

The lamentation of an opened abyss, as it were; the wounded earth cries out and voices are raised, deep as the bottomless pit, these are the depths of the abyss crying out.

Neuter. Feminine. Masculine.

To vent this cry I must exhaust myself.

Expelling not air but the very capacity to make sound. I draw up my human body before me. After casting the "EYE" of a fearful appraisal over it, I force it back into me point after point.

First the stomach. Silence must start in the stomach, left, right, at the spot where hernial congestion occurs, where surgeons operate.

In order to produce shouts of strength, the *Masculine* must first rely on this congestive point, must control the lungs bursting into breathing and the inrush of breath into the lungs.

Here, alas! it is just the opposite, and the war I want to wage stems from the war waged against me.

My *Neuter* harbours slaughter! An inflamed picture of slaughter nourishes my own war, you understand. My war is fed by war, hacking out its own war.

NEUTER. *Feminine. Masculine.* This neuter contains introversion, will-power lying in wait for war, flushing war out by the strength of its agitation.

At times this Neuter does not exist. A resting, an alight, in short, a spatial Neuter.

The void *stretches out* between two breaths, then it becomes like open ground stretching out.

Here, it is a strangled void. The choked void in the throat, where the very fury of the death-rattle has strangled all respiration.

Breath goes down into the belly,
creating its void,
launching it back up TO THE TOP OF THE LUNGS.

That means; in order to cry out I do not need strength, I merely need weakness, and will-power will spring from my weakness, will live to recharge my weakness with all demand's strength.

Yet, and this is the secret, *just as* IN THEATRE, strength does not emerge. The active masculine is oppressed. And it retains breathing's forceful will-power. It retains it within the body as a whole, while externally there is a picture of the disappearance of strength which the SENSES WILL BELIEVE THEY ARE WITNESSING.

Yet from my belly's void I reached the void threatening the top of my lungs.

From there, without any perceptible break, breathing went down to the small of my back, first with a feminine cry to the left, then to the right at the point where Chinese acupuncture pricks nervous fatigue, when the latter indicates the spleen or the viscera's mal-functioning, when it reveals poisoning.

Now I can fill my lungs with the sound of falls whose inflow would destroy my lungs, if the shout I wanted to give had not been a dream.

Massing the two points of the void on the belly, and from there, without passing into the lungs, concentrating these two points *a little above* the small of the back, they gave birth within me to the picture of that armed cry at war, that terrible underground cry.

I must fall to scream thus.

The scream of a warrior struck down, brushing past the broken walls with the sound of whirling mirrors.

I am falling.

I am falling but I am not afraid.

I express my fear with the sound of fury, in a solemn bellowing.

NEUTER. *Feminine. Masculine.*

The Neuter was heavy and settled. The Feminine is terrible, thundering, like the barking of a legendary mastiff, squat as cavernous columns, solid as the air which walls the cave's huge vaults.

I cry out in dreams,
but I know I am dreaming;
my will-power prevails
on BOTH SIDES OF DREAMS.
I scream within a bony frame, within the caverns of my rib cage, it assumes inordinate importance in my head's stupefied eyes.

But I must fall in order to scream this struck-down cry.
I fall into caves from which I cannot emerge, from which I will never emerge.
Nevermore *in the Masculine*.

I already said; the Masculine is nothing. It retains strength, but it entombs me in strength.
And outside this Masculine is a slap, an airy spectre, a sulphurous globule exploding in the water, the sigh from a closed mouth the instant it closes.
When all the breath has gone into the scream and none is left in the face. The closed, feminine face has just begun to dissociate itself from that mastiff's tremendous bellowing.

The falls begin here.
The cry I have just uttered *is* a dream.
But a dream which engulfs dreams.
I really am in a cave, I am breathing, suitably, O wonder, and I am the actor.
The air around me is vast but bottled up for the cavern is

Using breathing's hieroglyphics, I can rediscover a concept of divine theatre.

Mexico City, April 5, 1936.

POSTFACE

The theatre has been a major literary form since the great periods of ancient Greece, and, like poetry, a means of relating great events, of recording oral history, and of explaining man and his beliefs to himself. There is a dichotomy in a theatrical text because it can be performed both in public and in the theatre of the mind, and in the twentieth century it has also been possible to transfer the different forms of theatre to the screen. The mystique of Drama as a form of art lies in the antiquity, in its relationship to religion with which it has often been interlinked, and its potency as an educational force, as well as in its power to entertain an audience.

In the twentieth century a body of critical and evaluative writing has developed to look at the drama in all its aspects, especially its role as a factor in human evolution and as an enricher of life. Shaw, Stanislavsky, Piscator, Brecht, Grotowski, Kantor, Brook are only a few of those who have written about the theatre, but no one has been more wide-ranging and potent than Antonin Artaud, whose work and ideas have much influenced the last three of the above. Of his considerable body of work, most of which has appeared in English from the publishing imprint of Calder or is in preparation for future publication, *The Theatre and Its Double* is the best known and most important, central to Artaud's thinking. First published in Paris in February 1938, it brings together a

103

number of seminal short texts that he had compiled during the preceding six years.

Artaud in this extraordinary book likens the theatre to a plague, to the great plagues of history that have changed the course of human events, frustrating human progress and ambition and causing men and women to behave in a purely irrational manner. The fascination of the theatre, denounced by Saint Augustine for its power to drive men mad, lies in its potent ability to change the course of events: mankind likes to live in an illusory world of security, believing that the fabric of social living and an ordered society protects it from the terrors of the unknown; but this cosy security can be disrupted by invasion from without, civil war from within, disease or natural cataclysms such as earthquakes or volcanic eruptions. The role of the theatre must be to shake us out of complacency and our delusion of security. 'We are not free and the sky can still fall on our heads. And above all else, theatre is made to teach us this,' says Artaud in *No More Masterpieces*.

The phrase most often associated with Artaud is 'the theatre of cruelty', title of some of the central pages of *The Theatre and Its Double*, and it has been much misunderstood, often deliberately, especially by those looking for a weapon to attack his followers, those who have tried to put his theories into practice, such as Peter Brook, whose Theatre of Cruelty season at LAMDA in 1964 gave London a taste of Artaudian theatre in its most didactic form. For Artaud the theatre is pure poetry, disorientating the public from the certainties of everyday existence and taking away its certainties, making impossible its desire to ignore unpleasant reality and to bury its collective head in the sand. Artaud's concept is that the theatre must above all concern itself with subject matter that is relevant to the time, and not only not ignore the horrors of the moment, but, if possible, portray them as even more horrible, adding imagined horrors to existing ones. This means that acting styles must be extremely physical, as primitive as possible in showing the essential brutishness of man, and the theatrical canvas must be as rich as possible in employing every means that lie to hand in terms of decor, props; musical instruments, costumes and machinery. In short, Artaud's theatre is *total theatre*, a concept also envisaged by Piscator, Brecht and Claudel. We must remember that perhaps the greatest modern exponent of classical total theatre, from Aeschyllus to Claudel, has been Jean-Louis Barrault, who as actor and director started his career creating surrealist forms of theatre, working often under the direct influence of Artaud; Barrault brought the ideas and principles that he absorbed in those early years into forms of drama as diverse as Shakespeare, stage adaptations of Kafka's, Rabelais' and Voltaire's novels, the plays of Claudel, Beckett, Ionesco, Duras and other modern dramatists, and, of course, the great Greek classics. Peter Brook, usually working with more limited means and a polyglot multi-ethnic company of actors, has created his own versions of total theatre. Both directors have followed the basic Artaudian principle of disturbing the audience and forcing it out of its complacent certainty that it is only sitting in a theatre watching a play. In the case of Brook, before he moved to France, there was often vociferous political objection from part of the British public and the tabloid press, especially for his Theatre of Cruelty season and such plays as *The Marat/Sade* and *US*, the latter an attack on the American conduct of the Vietnam war. There have also been other Artaudian companies, such as Julian Beck's Living Theatre.

Artaud's theatrical ideas, when put into practice, can only have the effect of galvanising the audience, making it more alive and aware, sometimes politicising it, but above all bringing an element of magic into life, with pure poetry its major component. One must never forget that Artaud is a poet first and much of his most fascinating work is written in verse or poetic prose: the memorable phrase, the turning of a familiar symbol into a radical new image, the stretching of an extreme concept into an extravagance that makes it even more extreme, is typical of the man and must clinically lie at the roots of his madness as well as his genius.

> I am a poet, hearing voices that have no place in the world of
> ideas because there, where I am, there is nothing more to be
> thought.*

Artaud's insanity, which varied widely in degree and form
throughout his life, is of particular interest to psychiatry,
underlining the link between creative energy and abnormal states
of the mind. Neurasthenic in adolescence, in full revolt against his
sea-captain father and parental discipline, he was fortunate, after
being placed in a number of clinics, to find a psychiatrist who did
not try to turn him against his vocation for the theatre. Taken on
first by Lugné-Poe, the discoverer of Strindberg and Jarry, Artaud
studied for a time with Charles Dullin, one of the most influential
theatrical teachers of the day and a founder of the *Atelier* theatre
company in 1922. Artaud's literary career really began in 1923
with his long correspondence with Jacques Rivière, editor of the
Nouvelle Revue Française, who had refused his poems, but
nevertheless took an interest in the young man whose unusual
talent was looking for a shape into which to mould itself while he
was working as actor and student on all aspects of the theatrical
craft, simultaneously keeping up an astonishing and vast literary
activity.

   Artaud eventually left Dullin to start his own company together
with Roger Vitrac and Robert Aron, and this became the *Alfred
Jarry Theatre*. They were all associated with the surrealist
movement, and Artaud was even given the responsibility by André
Breton of editing the third issue of his journal, *La Révolution
Surréaliste,* but through the independence of the actions of Artaud
and his collaborators, in which Breton, the disciplinarian leader of
the 'official' surrealist group had little to say, they incurred his
anger and were expelled like so many others who had dared to
challenge his leadership and authority; but Artaud never

*From the preface to the first edition of his *Collected Works,*
written near the end of his life.

personally was anathemised, because of Breton's conviction that all madmen were inspired by a holy flame. By the end of the thirties Breton was in any case moving away from pure art and towards political commitment.

Between 1924 and 1935 Artaud worked in the cinema as well as in the theatre, and as an actor he has left us unforgettable images in such roles as the monk in Carl Dreyer's *Passion of Joan of Arc* and Marat in Abel Gance's *Napoléon*. His literary output never ceased and he always read widely, being attracted by many sources, and influenced by works as diverse as the plays of Shelley, Buchner's *Woyzeck*, the expressionistic theatre, the films of the Marx Brothers, the novels of the Marquis de Sade and his readings in history. The paintings of Bosch and Grunewald with their grim depictions of both real and imaginary cruelty all played a part in his concept of the dark night of the soul, the sombre vision of human existence that underlies his mystique, and is comparable to that of Baudelaire. His miserable years in the Asylum of Rodez, where he was sent at the time of the German occupation in 1940 until 1946, from which Adamov, who had himself been in a German concentration camp, organised his escape, increased the tragedy of his life and hastened his death in 1948 at the age of fifty-two.

His influence has grown ever since. Beckett and Ionesco owe something to him as well as the directors associated with total and poetic theatre, and later 'absurdist' playwrights like Fernando Arrabal have been indirectly influenced through them. In a century that has shown a savagery to equal any other in history, the concept of cruelty as a means of artistic concentration should not be so foreign or difficult to understand. It is not, as Artaud is careful to explain, a matter of bloodshed or sadism, martyred flesh or crucified enemies, but rather of a 'strict control and submission to necessity'. The presence of death always makes life more vivid and 'being alive always means the death of someone else.'

All of Artaud's work is interesting, even when disjointed and fragmentary, and there is great poetry and even genius in much of his writing, but it is *The Theatre and Its Double* that has always aroused the greatest interest. It remains ones of the key texts of theatrical writing. Artaud's life, like his work, has to be seen in the context of his extreme vividness of poetic utterance, of the triumph of his life-force over his death-wish, of an imagination overflowing with creativity and the kind of awareness that one associates with saints and mystics. His prose is always exciting and life-enhancing, because it is literature as well as exploration. His aim was always to take the theatre out of the context of entertainment and into that of education, but paradoxically it thereby becomes entertainment as well; ultimately it might be said that surface entertainment is essentially boring because it requires so little concentration, while real entertainment does the opposite, making audiences better able to cope with the complex and dangerous world we inhabit.

JOHN CALDER

108